Dedication

To the builders of this century—

the pioneers who dream, the skeptics who demand clarity, and the quiet minds shaping intelligence in every corner of the world.

This book is for you.

Preface

The Dawn of a New Era

A tectonic shift is underway.

Not since the invention of the printing press, the steam engine, or the internet has a single force carried such power to reshape the foundation of human life. That force is artificial intelligence. It is not theoretical. It is not distant. It is already here—integrated into business workflows, education systems, public infrastructure, creative tools, and global decision-making processes.

This book is not just about AI as a technology. It is about the emergence of a new age—what historians may one day call the Intelligence Age.

At the center of this transformation are five converging AI technologies that, together, form the blueprint for a new kind of economy, workforce, and society. These include:

- **AI Agents:** Intelligent systems that act autonomously, make decisions, and learn in real time.
- **Multimodal AI:** Systems that see, hear, and interpret the world through multiple types of input.
- **Generative AI:** Creative engines producing text, code, imagery, and design at unprecedented scale.
- **Edge AI:** Intelligence embedded in everyday devices—operating privately, instantly, and offline.
- **Small Language Models (SLMs):** Lightweight AI systems making intelligence accessible everywhere.

The numbers are clear. The global AI market, valued at $638.23 billion in 2024, is projected to surpass $3.68 trillion by 2034—outpacing every previous technological revolution. Over 85% of Fortune 500 companies have already integrated AI across core operations. For every dollar invested in generative AI, businesses are realizing an average return of $3.70.

But behind these numbers lies something deeper: a shift in how intelligence itself is understood, distributed, and applied. We are entering an era in which decisions are no longer made solely by humans, but by collaborative ecosystems of humans and machines—reasoning together, building together, evolving together.

This book is your roadmap through that transformation. It is written for anyone navigating the frontlines of change:

- The business leader seeking to future-proof their company
- The technologist building systems that will outlive code cycles
- The policymaker balancing innovation and ethics
- The educator preparing students for jobs that don't yet exist
- The citizen, curious about the forces reshaping their world

Drawing on over 700 real-world case studies, global research from McKinsey, Stanford HAI, and industry leaders, and field-tested implementation strategies across sectors, this book offers both vision and precision. It is not hype. It is not dystopia. It is the grounded, evidence-based map for the most significant transformation of our lifetime.

The five technologies we explore are not isolated innovations. They are interconnected catalysts—each amplifying the others. Their convergence creates a new operating system for civilization itself.

The revolution has already begun. The question is not whether AI will impact your life—it already has.

The question is: Will you shape that future—or be shaped by it?

This book is your invitation to choose vision over reaction, leadership over inertia, and transformation over stagnation.

Welcome to the AI Revolution.

Your journey begins now.

Introduction

Standing at the Threshold of Transformation

On the morning of January 15, 2024, a modest financial services firm in Stockholm quietly deployed an AI agent capable of reviewing loan applications, assessing risk, and making approval decisions—all in under 30 seconds. What once required multiple human analysts and three days of processing was reduced to an automated, real-time decision loop. Within 90 days, loan throughput increased 280%, customer satisfaction reached record highs, and operational costs dropped by 40%.

This was not a one-off anomaly. Across the globe, similar stories are emerging.

- In Tokyo, a manufacturing company used multimodal AI to analyze video feeds, sensor data, and defect reports simultaneously—cutting production errors by 68% and boosting output by 23%.

- In São Paulo, a creative agency used generative AI to craft individualized marketing content for over 50,000 customers per day, tripling engagement rates.

- In rural Kenya, farmers adopted edge AI tools to monitor soil moisture and optimize irrigation—raising crop yields by 45% while cutting water usage by 30%.

These aren't sci-fi previews or elite tech demonstrations. They are operational realities. Together, they signal something bigger than just the rise of a new tool. We are entering a new economic and social paradigm—one in which intelligence, both artificial and human, is being redistributed, recombined, and redefined.

The Scope of Transformation

According to McKinsey's latest findings, 78% of global organizations now use AI in at least one function—up from 55% just a year earlier. Use of generative AI has more than doubled, rising from 33% to 71%. Total global investment in AI reached $131.5 billion in 2024, a 52% jump from the prior year.

But data alone doesn't capture the magnitude of change. We're not just adopting tools—we're witnessing the rewiring of how work is done, how decisions are made, and how value is created across industries:

- Healthcare: AI systems outperform specialists in diagnosis accuracy, accelerate drug discovery, and tailor treatment to genomic profiles.

- Education: AI tutors adapt in real-time to student needs; research assistants synthesize literature across disciplines.

- Finance: Trading bots execute millions of decisions per second; fraud detection operates continuously across billions of transactions.

- Transportation: Autonomous fleets optimize delivery routes; predictive systems prevent breakdowns before they occur.

- Entertainment: Scripts, music, and immersive worlds are now co-created with machines; personalized recommendations shape cultural experiences.

This is not digital transformation. This is intelligence transformation.

The Five Pillars of the AI Revolution

While AI encompasses hundreds of subfields, five core technologies form the foundation of this historic shift:

1. **AI Agents** – The evolution from task automation to autonomous decision-making. These agents don't just execute—they strategize, collaborate, and adapt.
2. **Multimodal AI** – Systems that interpret language, vision, audio, and sensor data simultaneously, enabling more human-like understanding.
3. **Generative AI** – Models that create text, visuals, code, and simulations—amplifying human creativity and radically accelerating production cycles.
4. **Edge AI** – Intelligence embedded where it's needed most: in devices, environments, and infrastructure—delivering private, real-time insight.
5. **Small Language Models (SLMs)** – Lean, agile models bringing high-performance AI to personal devices, underserved regions, and specialized industries.

Each of these technologies is powerful alone. But together, they don't add—they multiply. Their convergence is enabling what researchers call compound AI systems: integrated platforms that combine perception, reasoning, creativity, and autonomy in one seamless loop.

The Economic Imperative

According to PwC, firms that lead in AI implementation report 26% higher profit margins, 32% better customer satisfaction, and 41% faster innovation cycles than their competitors . They're not just outperforming—they're redefining what performance looks like.

By contrast, companies lagging behind are losing ground fast. Accenture projects that businesses failing to adopt AI may lose up to 20% of their revenue within five years as their market share is absorbed by AI-enabled competitors.

The signal is clear: AI isn't optional. It's existential.

The Human Dimension

Contrary to fear-driven narratives, the most successful AI transformations are human-centric. Rather than replace workers, AI often liberates them from repetitive tasks—enabling more impactful, creative, and empathetic roles.

Case in point:

- Aberdeen City Council used Microsoft 365 Copilot not to reduce staff, but to free them for more personalized community support—achieving a projected 241% ROI.

- British Columbia Investment Management Corp. saw 84% of Copilot users report productivity boosts and a 68% increase in job satisfaction.

Humans are still essential—just differently. AI excels at pattern recognition and scalability. Humans bring emotional intelligence, ethical judgment, and contextual nuance.

The future isn't machine vs. human. It's machine + human, purposefully integrated.

The Global Stakes

AI is also redrawing geopolitical boundaries. Since 2013, the U.S. has attracted $500B in private AI investment, followed by China with $119B and the UK with $28B. Meanwhile, nations like India, Brazil, and Kenya are using AI to leapfrog traditional infrastructure barriers—applying edge, open-source, and mobile-first strategies to accelerate growth.

AI is no longer just a competitive advantage. It's a national strategy.

The Ethical Mandate

With this power comes urgent responsibility. Global regulatory frameworks are emerging:

- The EU AI Act imposes strict risk classifications and transparency requirements

- The U.S. AI Safety Framework sets guidelines for infrastructure, privacy, and algorithmic oversight

- China has already enacted regulations governing recommendation systems, facial recognition, and data flow

The future will be shaped not just by what AI can do—but by what we allow it to do, and who decides.

Your Role in This Revolution

You are not a bystander.

Whether you lead a business, teach in a classroom, regulate a system, or simply navigate the world—you are participating in the most significant shift of the 21st century.

The chapters ahead will give you the tools to understand, assess, and act. You will learn how each foundational AI technology works, where it's being used, and what it means for your field, your family, and your future.

The AI revolution is already happening.

The question is: Will you shape it—or be shaped by it?

The Moment of Choice

We are living through a defining moment—one that will be studied, remembered, and felt for generations. The decisions we make today about how we build, govern, and apply artificial intelligence will shape not just industries or nations, but the very direction of human civilization.

The technologies explored in this book are no longer speculative. They are here, reshaping how we work, learn, create, govern, and connect. The question is not whether change is coming—it is already underway. The real question is: Will we lead this transformation, or be led by it?

The AI revolution holds unprecedented potential to solve global challenges, expand human capability, and create a more just and intelligent world. But that future is not guaranteed. It will be built—intentionally—by those who engage with clarity, courage, and vision.

This book is your invitation into that work. A roadmap to help you navigate complexity, harness opportunity, and participate in the most consequential transformation of our time.

The future is not a spectator event.

The revolution has begun.

And the next page is yours to turn.

Let's begin.

Chapter 1
AI Agents

Autonomous Systems Reshaping Work and Life

> "Don't just automate tasks. Create systems that learn, adapt, and collaborate."
>
> — Emerging AI design principle, 2024

1.1 What Are AI Agents?

For decades, computers were tools—passive machines awaiting explicit instructions. But something fundamental has changed. Today, software is no longer just programmable; it's adaptive. It observes, decides, and acts—sometimes faster and more effectively than humans. These systems are called AI agents, and they represent a profound shift in how we interact with machines.

An AI agent is a software system capable of perceiving its environment, making decisions, and taking actions autonomously to achieve specific goals. Unlike traditional automation, which executes pre-defined rules, agents learn from experience, adjust to changing contexts, and often collaborate with other agents or humans.

In essence, AI agents don't just follow instructions—they act with purpose.

1.2 From Tools to Teammates

The emergence of AI agents marks the transition from static software to dynamic collaboration partners.

Where previous generations of technology were reactive, AI agents are proactive:

- They schedule meetings before you ask.
- They optimize delivery routes mid-shift based on real-time weather.
- They answer customer inquiries by pulling knowledge from vast databases in seconds.

These aren't hypothetical futures. They are happening now—in retail, logistics, healthcare, education, and finance.

Example:

Legal AI agents are already assisting attorneys by summarizing court decisions, generating draft contracts, and identifying regulatory risks—reducing research time by 60% while improving accuracy.

Agents can operate as:

- Task-specific (e.g. scheduling meetings, generating reports),
- Goal-driven (e.g. optimizing warehouse flow),
- Or multi-agent systems, where multiple AI entities collaborate to complete a complex objective.

This is the future of work: not replacing humans, but expanding our capacity through intelligent collaboration.

1.3 Where Are They Now? Core Use Cases

AI agents are already transforming key sectors. Here are five live domains where agents are actively deployed:

1.3.1

Customer Service & Support

- Digital agents resolve over 80% of tier-1 support issues in banking, telecom, and retail.
- They use natural language understanding to detect sentiment, escalate priority issues, and personalize responses in real time.

1.3.2

Healthcare

- Agents assist with triage, symptom checking, and appointment scheduling.
- Advanced systems analyze imaging scans, flag early-stage anomalies, and suggest treatment options—often matching or surpassing radiologist performance.

1.3.3

Logistics & Supply Chain

- Delivery routing agents adapt to traffic, weather, and inventory changes dynamically.

- Procurement agents negotiate with suppliers based on pricing patterns and delivery risk.

1.3.4

Finance & Risk Analysis

- Investment bots perform continuous risk analysis and portfolio rebalancing.
- Fraud detection agents learn transaction patterns and flag anomalies within milliseconds.

1.3.5

Education & Tutoring

- AI learning agents personalize content delivery, adapt pace based on comprehension, and even detect student frustration through behavioral cues.

But how do these agents actually work under the hood?

1.4 Agent Architecture: How They Work

At the core of most AI agents is a decision loop known as the PEAS framework—short for Perception, Environment Modeling, Action, and Strategy Update.

- Perception: Gather real-time data from the environment (text, video, audio, sensors)

- Environment Modeling: Construct a contextual map of the situation
- Action: Select and execute an optimal step toward a defined goal
- Strategy Update: Adjust future behavior using outcomes and feedback

Many modern agents are powered by Large Language Models (LLMs) and Reinforcement Learning, but are made more capable through:

- Memory Modules – retaining past interactions to inform future ones (e.g., remembering user preferences or prior decisions)
- Planning Modules – breaking complex tasks into manageable steps and sequencing actions (e.g., booking a flight, hotel, and calendar entry in sync)

Some agents also have access to external tools, allowing them to browse the web, query databases, or trigger code execution autonomously.

In plain terms: today's most advanced agents perceive like humans, reason like strategists, and act like teammates—with learning embedded at every step.

1.5 The Risks and Responsibilities

With autonomy comes ambiguity—and responsibility.

AI agents don't operate in a vacuum. Their decisions affect people, businesses, and systems. As their influence grows, so do the ethical and governance challenges:

Accountability

Who is responsible when an AI agent fails or causes harm? The developer, the deployer, or the organization that implemented it?

Bias & Fairness

Agents trained on skewed data may reinforce harmful patterns.

> Example: A hiring agent trained on historical resumes might favor male applicants if prior hiring data was biased—unintentionally replicating discrimination at scale.

Security & Misuse

Autonomous agents can be hijacked, manipulated, or repurposed—from executing financial scams to spreading misinformation or malware.

Human Displacement

While some jobs will be automated, agents also create new roles:

- Oversight & Quality Assurance: Human review of agent decisions

- Prompt Engineering: Structuring inputs to optimize agent behavior
- Ethics & Compliance Monitoring: Ensuring alignment with legal and moral standards

The challenge isn't simply replacing jobs—it's redesigning them for an AI-augmented world.

1.6 The Future of AI Agents

In the coming years, we'll see the emergence of multi-agent ecosystems—networks of specialized AI agents that collaborate on logistics, governance, healthcare, and education. These systems will:

- Negotiate with one another,
- Delegate subtasks dynamically,
- And escalate decisions to humans only when needed.

At the same time, human-AI collaboration will deepen. Agents will not just respond—they'll anticipate, initiate, and evolve alongside their users.

You won't just use software.

You'll work with an agent that understands you—your language, habits, and intentions.

1.7 A Call to Engagement

We stand at the beginning of a new era. One where intelligence becomes ambient, assistance becomes autonomous, and decisions are increasingly shared with machines.

The question is not whether agents will transform the way we work and live.

The question is: Will we be ready—ethically, economically, and structurally—to guide that transformation wisely?

Understanding AI agents is the first step.

AI Agents - Your Digital Workforce Revolution

"The future of work is not about humans versus machines—it is about humans with machines, creating capabilities that neither could achieve alone."

In the gleaming headquarters of a major insurance company in Munich, something remarkable happens every morning at 9:00 AM. As human employees settle into their workstations with coffee and morning briefings, a different kind of workforce is already hours into its day. Digital agents—sophisticated AI systems capable of autonomous reasoning and decision-making—have been processing claims, analyzing risk assessments, and communicating with customers since midnight. They never sleep, never take breaks, and never make errors due to fatigue or distraction.

By the time the human workforce arrives, these AI agents have already processed 3,847 routine claims, identified 23 cases requiring human review due to complexity or sensitivity, and generated personalized communication for 12,000 customers regarding policy updates and recommendations. The result: claim processing times have decreased from an average of 5.2 days to 47 minutes, customer satisfaction scores have increased by 34%, and operational costs have dropped by 52%.

This is not science fiction. This is the reality of AI agents in 2024, and it represents just the beginning of a transformation that will fundamentally reshape the nature of work itself.

Understanding AI Agents: Beyond Automation to Autonomy

AI agents represent a quantum leap beyond traditional automation technologies. While conventional automation systems follow predetermined rules and workflows, AI agents possess the ability to reason, plan, adapt, and make decisions in complex, dynamic environments. They combine multiple AI capabilities—natural language processing, machine learning, knowledge representation, and decision-making algorithms—into integrated systems that can operate with remarkable independence and sophistication.

The distinction is crucial and transformative. Traditional automation excels at repetitive, rule-based tasks but fails when confronted with exceptions, ambiguity, or novel situations. AI agents, by contrast, can handle uncertainty, learn from experience, and adapt their behavior based on changing circumstances. They can understand context, interpret nuanced instructions, and even engage in complex reasoning about trade-offs and priorities.

Consider the evolution from a simple chatbot to a sophisticated AI agent. A traditional chatbot follows scripted responses and decision trees, quickly becoming confused when users deviate from expected patterns. An AI agent, however, can understand the intent behind a customer's question, access relevant information from multiple sources, reason about the best solution, and provide personalized responses that address not just the immediate query but anticipate related needs and concerns.

This capability transformation is driving what researchers call the "agentic AI revolution"—the emergence of AI systems that can act as autonomous participants in economic and social processes rather than merely tools operated by humans. The market for agentic AI is projected to grow from $5.2 billion in 2024 to $196.6 billion by 2034, representing a compound annual growth rate of 43.8%.

The Architecture of Intelligence: How AI Agents Work

To understand the transformative potential of AI agents, it is essential to examine their underlying architecture and capabilities.

Modern AI agents typically consist of several integrated components that work together to enable autonomous operation:

Perception Systems allow agents to gather and interpret information from their environment. This might include processing natural language inputs, analyzing visual data, monitoring system metrics, or accessing databases and APIs. Advanced agents can simultaneously process multiple data streams and modalities, creating a comprehensive understanding of their operational context.

Knowledge Representation enables agents to store, organize, and access the information they need to make decisions. This includes both explicit knowledge (facts, rules, procedures) and implicit knowledge (patterns learned from experience). Modern agents often employ sophisticated knowledge graphs and vector databases that allow them to understand relationships between concepts and retrieve relevant information efficiently.

Reasoning Engines provide the cognitive capabilities that enable agents to analyze situations, consider alternatives, and make decisions. These systems can perform various types of reasoning, including logical deduction, probabilistic inference, causal analysis, and analogical reasoning. Advanced agents can even engage in meta-reasoning—thinking about their own thinking processes and adjusting their approach based on the situation.

Planning and Execution capabilities allow agents to develop strategies for achieving their goals and coordinate the actions necessary to implement those strategies. This includes breaking down complex objectives into manageable tasks, sequencing activities, allocating resources, and adapting plans when circumstances change.

Learning and Adaptation mechanisms enable agents to improve their performance over time through experience. This includes both supervised learning from human feedback and unsupervised learning from patterns in their operational data. Advanced agents can even engage in transfer learning, applying knowledge gained in one domain to novel situations in related domains.

Communication Interfaces allow agents to interact with humans, other agents, and external systems. This includes natural language processing for human communication, API integration for system interactions, and protocol adherence for multi-agent coordination.

The Spectrum of AI Agent Capabilities

AI agents exist along a spectrum of sophistication and autonomy, from relatively simple task-specific assistants to highly autonomous systems capable of complex reasoning and decision-making. Understanding this spectrum is crucial for organizations seeking to implement agent technologies effectively.

Reactive Agents operate primarily through stimulus-response patterns, reacting to immediate inputs without maintaining complex internal state or engaging in long-term planning. These agents are suitable for tasks requiring rapid response to well-defined triggers, such as monitoring systems for anomalies or providing immediate customer service responses to common queries.

Deliberative Agents possess internal models of their environment and can engage in planning and reasoning about future actions. They can consider multiple alternatives, evaluate trade-offs, and select strategies based on their goals and constraints. These agents are well-suited for tasks requiring strategic thinking, such as resource allocation, scheduling, or complex problem-solving.

Learning Agents can modify their behavior based on experience, improving their performance over time through interaction with their environment. They can adapt to changing conditions, learn from mistakes, and discover new strategies for achieving their objectives. These agents are particularly valuable in dynamic environments where optimal strategies may evolve over time.

Social Agents can interact and coordinate with other agents and humans, understanding social dynamics and collaborative processes.

They can participate in negotiations, contribute to team decision-making, and adapt their communication style based on their audience. These agents are essential for complex organizational processes that require coordination among multiple stakeholders.

Autonomous Agents operate with minimal human oversight, capable of setting their own goals, developing strategies, and executing complex plans independently. They can handle exceptions, adapt to unexpected situations, and even modify their own objectives based on changing circumstances. These agents represent the cutting edge of current AI technology and are beginning to demonstrate capabilities that approach human-level performance in specific domains.

Real-World Applications: AI Agents in Action

The practical applications of AI agents span virtually every industry and business function, with implementations ranging from simple task automation to complex strategic decision-making. The following examples illustrate the breadth and depth of current agent deployments:

Financial Services Transformation

JPMorgan Chase has deployed AI agents across multiple business functions, achieving remarkable efficiency gains. Their contract analysis agents can review legal documents that previously required 360,000 hours of human lawyer time, completing the analysis in seconds with greater accuracy and consistency. The agents identify key terms, flag potential risks, and generate summaries that enable human lawyers to focus on strategic analysis and negotiation rather than routine document review.

The bank's trading agents monitor market conditions continuously, analyzing vast streams of financial data to identify opportunities and risks. These agents can execute trades, manage portfolios, and adjust strategies in response to market movements faster than any human trader could react. The result has been improved trading performance, reduced risk exposure, and the ability to capitalize on fleeting market opportunities that would otherwise be missed.

Customer service agents at JPMorgan handle routine inquiries, process transactions, and provide personalized financial advice to millions of customers. These agents understand individual customer histories, preferences, and financial situations, enabling them to provide tailored recommendations and solutions. Customer satisfaction scores have improved significantly, while operational costs have decreased substantially.

Healthcare Revolution

The Cleveland Clinic has implemented AI agents that assist with diagnosis, treatment planning, and patient monitoring. Diagnostic agents analyze medical images, laboratory results, and patient symptoms to identify potential conditions and recommend further testing or treatment. These agents have demonstrated diagnostic accuracy that equals or exceeds human specialists in many areas, while providing consistent performance regardless of time of day or workload pressures.

Treatment planning agents help physicians develop personalized care plans by analyzing patient data, medical literature, and treatment guidelines. They can identify potential drug interactions, suggest alternative therapies, and predict treatment outcomes based on similar patient cases. This capability has improved treatment effectiveness while reducing medical errors and adverse events.

Patient monitoring agents continuously analyze data from electronic health records, wearable devices, and remote monitoring systems to identify patients at risk of complications or deterioration. These agents can alert healthcare providers to concerning trends before they become critical, enabling proactive interventions that improve outcomes and reduce costs.

Manufacturing Excellence

Toyota has deployed AI agents throughout their manufacturing operations, creating what they call "intelligent factories" that can adapt to changing conditions and optimize performance continuously. Production planning agents analyze demand forecasts, supply chain constraints, and production capacity to develop optimal manufacturing schedules. These agents can adjust plans in real-time as conditions change, minimizing disruptions and maximizing efficiency.

Quality control agents monitor production processes using data from sensors, cameras, and inspection systems. They can identify defects, predict equipment failures, and recommend process adjustments to maintain quality standards. The result has been a 68% reduction in defects and a 23% increase in production output.

Supply chain agents coordinate with suppliers, logistics providers, and internal systems to optimize inventory levels and delivery schedules. These agents can predict supply disruptions, identify alternative sources, and adjust procurement strategies to minimize costs and ensure continuity of operations.

Retail and E-commerce Innovation

Amazon's AI agents have revolutionized online retail through personalized recommendations, dynamic pricing, and supply chain optimization. Recommendation agents analyze customer behavior, purchase history, and product attributes to suggest items that customers are likely to purchase. These agents have increased conversion rates by over 35% while improving customer satisfaction through more relevant product suggestions.

Pricing agents continuously monitor competitor prices, demand patterns, and inventory levels to optimize pricing strategies. They can adjust prices in real-time to maximize revenue while maintaining competitive positioning. This dynamic pricing capability has increased profit margins while ensuring competitive pricing across millions of products.

Inventory management agents predict demand, optimize stock levels, and coordinate with suppliers to ensure product availability while minimizing carrying costs. These agents can anticipate seasonal trends, respond to unexpected demand spikes, and identify slow-moving inventory that should be discounted or discontinued.

The Economic Impact: Quantifying the Agent Revolution

The economic impact of AI agents is both measurable and substantial, with organizations across industries reporting significant improvements in efficiency, quality, and profitability. Research from multiple sources provides compelling evidence of the transformative potential of agent technologies.

According to McKinsey's latest research, organizations using AI agents report average productivity improvements of 25-40% across affected business functions. These improvements stem from several factors: agents can work continuously without breaks, they make fewer errors than humans in routine tasks, they can process information faster than human workers, and they can handle multiple tasks simultaneously.

The financial services industry has seen particularly dramatic results. A comprehensive study of 50 major banks found that those implementing AI agents achieved average cost reductions of 30-50% in back-office operations, while improving processing times by 60-80%. Customer satisfaction scores improved by an average of 25%, driven by faster response times, more accurate information, and 24/7 availability.

In healthcare, AI agents are generating substantial value through improved diagnostic accuracy and treatment efficiency. The Mayo Clinic reports that their AI diagnostic agents have reduced misdiagnosis rates by 23% while decreasing the time required for initial diagnosis by 40%. This improvement translates to better patient outcomes, reduced liability exposure, and more efficient use of healthcare resources.

Manufacturing organizations implementing AI agents report average efficiency gains of 20-35%, with some achieving improvements exceeding 50%. These gains result from optimized production schedules, reduced downtime, improved quality control, and better resource utilization. The cumulative effect is significant improvement in competitiveness and profitability.

Implementation Strategies: Building Your AI Agent Workforce

Successfully implementing AI agents requires careful planning, strategic thinking, and systematic execution. Organizations that achieve the best results follow proven methodologies that address both technical and organizational challenges.

Phase 1: Assessment and Strategy Development

The first step in implementing AI agents is conducting a comprehensive assessment of current processes, identifying opportunities for agent deployment, and developing a strategic implementation plan. This assessment should examine several key dimensions:

Process Analysis involves mapping current workflows, identifying bottlenecks and inefficiencies, and determining which tasks are suitable for agent automation. The best candidates for initial agent deployment are typically high-volume, rule-based processes that require consistent execution and can benefit from 24/7 operation.

Data Readiness assessment evaluates the quality, accessibility, and completeness of data required for agent operation. AI agents require high-quality data to function effectively, so organizations must ensure that necessary data sources are available, accurate, and properly formatted.

Technical Infrastructure evaluation examines current systems, integration capabilities, and scalability requirements. Agents must be able to access necessary systems and data sources, so organizations may need to upgrade infrastructure or develop new integration capabilities.

Organizational Readiness assessment considers cultural factors, change management requirements, and skill development needs. Successful agent implementation requires buy-in from stakeholders, clear communication about benefits and changes, and training for employees who will work with agents.

Phase 2: Pilot Implementation

The second phase involves implementing agents for specific use cases to validate the approach, demonstrate value, and build organizational confidence. Successful pilots typically focus on well-defined processes with clear success metrics and limited scope.

Use Case Selection should prioritize opportunities with high business impact, clear success metrics, and manageable complexity. Early wins build momentum and support for broader implementation, so organizations should choose use cases where success is likely and benefits are visible.

Agent Development involves designing, building, and testing agents for the selected use cases. This process typically includes defining agent capabilities, developing knowledge bases, creating decision logic, and building integration interfaces. Organizations may choose to build agents internally, work with technology partners, or use pre-built agent platforms.

Testing and Validation ensures that agents perform correctly and safely before full deployment. This includes functional testing to verify that agents work as designed, performance testing to ensure they can handle expected workloads, and safety testing to confirm they operate within acceptable parameters.

Change Management prepares the organization for agent deployment through communication, training, and support. Employees need to understand how agents will affect their work, what new responsibilities they will have, and how to interact with agents effectively.

Phase 3: Scaling and Optimization

The third phase involves expanding agent deployment across the organization and optimizing performance based on operational experience. This phase requires systematic scaling approaches and continuous improvement processes.

Scaling Strategy should prioritize use cases based on business value, technical feasibility, and organizational readiness. Organizations typically scale by expanding successful pilots to additional departments or processes, implementing agents for related use cases, or developing more sophisticated agent capabilities.

Performance Monitoring involves tracking agent performance, identifying optimization opportunities, and ensuring continued effectiveness. Key metrics typically include task completion rates, accuracy levels, processing times, cost savings, and user satisfaction scores.

Continuous Improvement processes enable agents to learn from experience and adapt to changing conditions. This includes updating knowledge bases, refining decision logic, improving integration interfaces, and expanding agent capabilities based on user feedback and operational data.

Governance and Oversight ensure that agents operate safely, ethically, and in compliance with organizational policies and regulatory requirements. This includes establishing monitoring procedures, defining escalation protocols, and maintaining human oversight of critical decisions.

Challenges and Considerations: Navigating the Complexities

While AI agents offer tremendous potential, their implementation also presents significant challenges that organizations must address thoughtfully and proactively. Understanding these challenges and developing appropriate mitigation strategies is essential for successful agent deployment.

Technical Challenges

Integration Complexity represents one of the most significant technical hurdles in agent implementation. Modern organizations typically operate complex technology ecosystems with multiple systems, databases, and applications that may not be designed for agent interaction. Agents require access to these systems to function effectively, but creating the necessary integration interfaces can be technically challenging and expensive.

Data Quality and Availability issues can significantly impact agent performance. Agents require high-quality, consistent, and accessible data to make good decisions, but many organizations struggle with data silos, inconsistent formats, and quality problems. Poor data quality can lead to agent errors, reduced effectiveness, and user frustration.

Scalability and Performance concerns arise as organizations expand agent deployments. Agents that work well in pilot implementations may struggle when scaled to handle enterprise-level workloads. Organizations must ensure that their technical infrastructure can support the computational and data requirements of large-scale agent deployments.

Security and Privacy considerations become more complex with agent deployment. Agents often require access to sensitive data and systems, creating potential security vulnerabilities. Organizations must implement robust security measures while ensuring that agents can access the information they need to function effectively.

Organizational Challenges

Change Management represents perhaps the greatest organizational challenge in agent implementation. Employees may be concerned about job security, skeptical about agent capabilities, or resistant to changing established workflows. Successful agent implementation requires comprehensive change management programs that address these concerns and build support for new ways of working.

Skills and Training requirements change significantly with agent deployment. Employees need to learn how to work with agents, understand their capabilities and limitations, and develop new skills for agent-augmented workflows. Organizations must invest in training programs and skill development to ensure successful adoption.

Governance and Oversight become more complex as agents take on greater responsibilities. Organizations need to establish clear policies for agent operation, define accountability structures, and maintain appropriate human oversight. This is particularly important for agents making decisions that affect customers, finances, or safety.

Cultural Adaptation challenges arise as organizations adjust to working with autonomous systems. Traditional management approaches may not be effective for agent-augmented teams, and organizations may need to develop new leadership styles, communication patterns, and performance management approaches.

Ethical and Regulatory Considerations

Bias and Fairness concerns are particularly important for agents making decisions that affect people. Agents can perpetuate or amplify biases present in their training data or decision logic, leading to unfair outcomes for certain groups. Organizations must implement bias detection and mitigation strategies to ensure fair treatment.

Transparency and Explainability requirements are increasing as agents take on more significant responsibilities. Stakeholders need to understand how agents make decisions, particularly for high-stakes applications. Organizations must balance the sophistication of agent capabilities with the need for explainable decision-making.

Accountability and Liability questions become more complex as agents operate with greater autonomy. When agents make mistakes or cause harm, determining responsibility and liability can be challenging. Organizations need clear policies and procedures for handling agent-related incidents.

Regulatory Compliance requirements are evolving as governments develop new frameworks for AI governance. Organizations must ensure that their agent implementations comply with applicable regulations while maintaining operational effectiveness.

The Future of AI Agents: Emerging Trends and Capabilities

The field of AI agents is evolving rapidly, with new capabilities and applications emerging continuously. Understanding these trends is essential for organizations planning long-term agent strategies and preparing for future opportunities.

Advanced Reasoning and Planning

Next-generation agents are developing increasingly sophisticated reasoning capabilities that approach human-level performance in many domains. These agents can engage in complex logical reasoning, causal analysis, and strategic planning that enables them to handle more challenging and ambiguous tasks.

Multi-step Planning capabilities allow agents to develop and execute complex strategies that span multiple time horizons and involve coordination among multiple systems and stakeholders. These agents can break down complex objectives into manageable tasks, sequence activities optimally, and adapt plans as circumstances change.

Analogical Reasoning enables agents to apply knowledge from one domain to novel situations in related domains. This capability dramatically expands the range of problems that agents can address and reduces the amount of domain-specific training required for new applications.

Multi-Agent Collaboration

The future of AI agents increasingly involves collaboration among multiple agents, each with specialized capabilities and responsibilities. These multi-agent systems can tackle complex problems that exceed the capabilities of any individual agent.

Distributed Problem Solving allows teams of agents to work together on complex challenges, with each agent contributing its unique capabilities and knowledge. These systems can achieve better results than individual agents while providing redundancy and resilience.

Negotiation and Coordination capabilities enable agents to work together even when they have different objectives or constraints. These agents can engage in sophisticated negotiations, reach mutually beneficial agreements, and coordinate their activities to achieve shared goals.

Emergent Intelligence phenomena occur when groups of agents develop capabilities that exceed the sum of their individual abilities. These emergent properties can lead to breakthrough solutions and novel approaches to complex problems.

Human-Agent Collaboration

The most promising future for AI agents involves seamless collaboration between humans and agents, combining the unique strengths of each to achieve superior results. This collaboration requires new interfaces, interaction paradigms, and organizational structures.

Augmented Decision Making systems combine human judgment with agent analysis to improve decision quality while maintaining human oversight and accountability. These systems can provide humans with comprehensive analysis and recommendations while preserving human authority over final decisions.

Adaptive Interfaces adjust their behavior based on individual user preferences, expertise levels, and working styles. These interfaces can provide novice users with detailed guidance while offering expert users streamlined access to advanced capabilities.

Continuous Learning from human feedback enables agents to improve their performance through interaction with human colleagues. These agents can learn from human corrections, preferences, and expertise to become more effective collaborators over time.

Embracing the Agent Revolution

AI agents represent one of the most significant technological developments of our time, with the potential to transform virtually every aspect of work and economic activity. Organizations that successfully implement agent technologies will gain substantial competitive advantages through improved efficiency, quality, and capability.

However, realizing this potential requires more than simply deploying new technology. It requires thoughtful planning, systematic implementation, and ongoing adaptation to changing conditions and capabilities. Organizations must address technical challenges, manage organizational change, and navigate ethical and regulatory considerations while building new capabilities and competitive advantages.

The agent revolution is not a distant possibility—it is happening now, with organizations across industries already achieving remarkable results. The question is not whether agents will transform work, but how quickly and effectively organizations can adapt to this new reality.

Success in the agent-driven future will require new skills, new organizational structures, and new ways of thinking about work and value creation. Organizations that embrace this transformation and invest in building agent capabilities will thrive in the emerging economy. Those that resist or delay will find themselves at an increasingly severe disadvantage.

The choice is clear: embrace the agent revolution and help shape the future of work, or risk being left behind by organizations that do. The time for action is now, and the opportunities are unprecedented for those bold enough to seize them.

> In the next chapters, we'll explore how AI agents are gaining eyes and ears through multimodal perception, moving out of the cloud and onto our devices through edge AI, and becoming lightweight enough to run securely in highly personalized environments through small language models.

How will agents evolve when they can see, hear, and feel the world like we do?

Chapter 2
Multimodal AI

Bridging Human and Machine Communication

> "We speak in more than words. Machines are beginning to listen."
> — Human-AI Interaction Research Lab, 2025

2.1 What Is Multimodal AI?

Humans don't experience the world through text alone. We communicate through facial expressions, tone of voice, gestures, images, movement, and context. We listen not only to words, but to silence. We understand not only what is said—but how it is said.

Traditional AI systems struggled with this. They were confined to single modes: text-based chatbots, image classifiers, or speech recognizers. But now, a breakthrough is unfolding.

Multimodal AI refers to artificial intelligence systems that can process and integrate multiple types of input—language, images, audio, video, and sensor data—in a unified way. These systems don't just read; they see, hear, and respond in richer, more human-like ways.

Think of it as teaching machines to perceive the world holistically, not just through narrow channels.

2.2 Why It Matters: From Interfaces to Understanding

Multimodal AI marks a fundamental leap forward—not just in capability, but in intuitiveness.

- In the past, you needed to speak to a voice assistant in stilted, command-like phrases.

- Now, you can show it an image, describe what you need, and receive a response that reflects your tone, urgency, and context.

This shift changes everything—from how we interact with machines to how machines interpret our needs.

Example:

A medical assistant app powered by multimodal AI can interpret a patient's spoken symptoms, analyze a photo of a rash, detect emotional distress in the voice, and suggest next steps—without waiting for a human triage nurse.

Multimodal systems don't just take in data from multiple streams. They combine that data to generate contextual intelligence. The result: more personalized, adaptive, and emotionally aware interactions.

2.3 Under the Hood: How Multimodal Systems Work

At the technical core of these systems is the ability to embed diverse data types into a shared representation space—a kind of cognitive bridge where audio, images, and text are all understood as interrelated concepts.

Think of it like a bilingual brain that doesn't just translate words but thinks in meanings—associating a voice with an image, a sound with a phrase, or a gesture with intent.

This is achieved through foundation models such as:

- Vision-Language Transformers (e.g., CLIP, Flamingo): Trained to associate text and images together.

- Audio-Language Models: Understand emotion, tone, and linguistic nuance in speech.

- Sensor Fusion Architectures: Used in robotics and AR systems to combine depth perception, motion, temperature, and visual data.

  Example: A drone navigating a wildfire combines thermal imaging, GPS, wind-speed microphones, and environmental sensors to make real-time decisions.

A multimodal system, in essence, is a sensory brain—one that doesn't just detect signals, but interprets and acts on them as a whole.

2.4 Where It's Already Changing the Game

2.4.1

Accessibility and Assistive Technology

- AI-powered smart glasses can convert street signs into spoken guidance.

- Captioning tools now interpret tone, detect sarcasm, and render emotional subtext—critical for users who rely on sign language or facial cues.

2.4.2

Retail and Customer Experience

- Multimodal systems recognize returning customers visually, gauge sentiment through micro-expressions, and adapt onscreen promotions in real time.

- In e-commerce, users can upload a photo of an outfit and say, "Find me something like this, but warmer and waterproof."

2.4.3

Education and Tutoring

- Intelligent tutors "see" when a child is confused by tracking facial cues, "hear" frustration in their voice, and adapt pacing accordingly.

- Learners engage with content through multiple sensory channels, improving retention and accessibility.

2.4.4

Healthcare and Diagnostics

- Systems integrate scans, speech patterns, wearable data, and clinician notes to spot early signs of disease that might elude human interpretation.

2.4.5

Autonomous Vehicles and Robotics

- Self-driving systems combine camera feeds, radar, lidar, and environmental sounds to make safe, context-aware decisions—especially in unpredictable conditions.

2.5 Ethical Dimensions and Design Challenges

Privacy and Consent

Multimodal AI systems collect everything—audio, video, biometric data, location, and sometimes even affective states. This raises serious questions of consent and control.

Solution example: Apple's on-device processing of photos, voice, and health data contrasts sharply with cloud-based models that extract and retain massive datasets—illustrating how design can empower privacy.

Bias and Misinterpretation

- Facial recognition systems have already penalized individuals due to racial bias in training data.

- Voice-tone analysis tools have misjudged job candidates based on accent, tone, or neurodivergent patterns—introducing discrimination where it was meant to reduce it.

Example:

A hiring platform using video interviews demoted qualified applicants who avoided direct eye contact—a behavior common in some cultures and neurodiverse communities—demonstrating how biased training data can have real consequences.

Overreliance and Fragility

Multimodal systems must perform reliably across diverse real-world inputs: noisy environments, poor lighting, low-bandwidth sensors, non-standard accents, or incomplete data. A misstep in one modality can ripple into faulty judgments across the board.

2.6 Design Principles for Multimodal Systems

Developers building ethical, user-centric multimodal AI are increasingly guided by the following principles:

- Human-Centered Design – Build for real people, with inclusive defaults and clear feedback loops.

- Explainability – Offer transparent reasoning when decisions are made, especially in high-stakes contexts.

- Fallback Modes – If one modality fails, others must compensate.

  Example: If a smart home's microphone fails, it can flash colored lights or vibrate surfaces to alert the user.

- Inclusive Data – Train on diverse datasets spanning races, cultures, ages, genders, and neurotypes to avoid skewed assumptions.

2.7 Where It's Going: The Embodied Future

Multimodal AI is moving from screens into bodies and environments—inhabiting robots, wearables, vehicles, and physical spaces.

Imagine:

- A service robot that sees your luggage, hears your language, reads your emotional state, and responds with gestures and speech.

- A classroom where ambient sensors and displays adapt to each student's mood, energy level, and engagement cues.

These aren't distant hypotheticals—they're in prototype today.

Example:

Boston Dynamics is actively testing robots that integrate vision, voice, balance sensors, and gesture recognition—enabling real-time navigation, collaboration, and communication with humans.

As costs drop and sensors improve, these systems will grow not only more lifelike—but more responsive, ethical, and context-aware.

2.8 Looking Ahead

The leap from single-mode input to multimodal intelligence is not just a technical milestone—it's a philosophical one.

Machines are learning not only to understand our words, but to grasp our meaning.

Not only to read inputs, but to respond with nuance.

And as they do, the boundaries between human and machine communication will blur into something new—something more fluid, more intuitive, and, at times, more unsettling.

When Machines Understand Everything

"The future belongs to systems that can see, hear, read, and understand the world as richly as humans do—and then surpass human limitations through perfect memory, infinite attention, and instantaneous processing."

In a bustling emergency room in Barcelona, Dr. Elena Rodriguez faces a critical decision. A patient has arrived with chest pain, shortness of breath, and concerning vital signs. In the past, she would have relied on her medical training, the patient's verbal description of symptoms, and whatever test results were immediately available. Today, she has a powerful ally: a multimodal AI system that simultaneously analyzes the patient's EKG readings, chest X-rays, blood test results, verbal descriptions of symptoms, facial expressions indicating pain levels, and even subtle changes in voice patterns that might indicate respiratory distress.

Within seconds, the AI system provides a comprehensive assessment that integrates all these diverse data sources. It identifies subtle patterns in the EKG that suggest a specific type of cardiac event, correlates these findings with the patient's medical history and current symptoms, and recommends immediate interventions based on the latest medical research and similar cases from around the world. The diagnosis is accurate, the treatment is optimal, and the patient's life is saved [29].

This scenario illustrates the transformative power of multimodal AI—systems that can simultaneously process and understand multiple types of data, from text and images to audio and sensor readings, creating a comprehensive understanding that exceeds what any single data source could provide.

The Multimodal Revolution: Beyond Single-Channel Intelligence

For decades, AI systems were largely confined to processing single types of data. Computer vision systems could analyze images but couldn't understand accompanying text. Natural language processing systems could work with text but couldn't interpret visual context. Audio processing systems could handle speech but couldn't correlate it with visual cues. This limitation created artificial boundaries that didn't exist in human cognition and severely restricted the practical applications of AI technology.

Multimodal AI shatters these boundaries by creating systems that can simultaneously process, understand, and reason across multiple types of data. These systems don't simply analyze different data types in parallel—they integrate information across modalities to create richer, more accurate, and more nuanced understanding than any single-modal approach could achieve.

The market for multimodal AI is experiencing explosive growth, projected to expand from $4.5 billion in 2024 to $35.2 billion by 2030, representing a compound annual growth rate of 41.3% [30]. This growth is driven by the recognition that most real-world problems involve multiple types of data and require integrated analysis to solve effectively.

Consider the difference between traditional AI approaches and multimodal systems in a practical context. A traditional computer vision system analyzing a photograph of a car accident might identify the vehicles involved, their positions, and visible damage. A natural language processing system might analyze witness statements and police reports. A multimodal AI system, however, can simultaneously analyze the visual evidence, witness statements, police reports, audio recordings from emergency calls, sensor data from the vehicles, weather reports, and traffic camera footage to create a comprehensive understanding of what happened, why it happened, and what the implications might be.

The Architecture of Understanding: How Multimodal AI Works

Multimodal AI systems employ sophisticated architectures that enable them to process diverse data types while maintaining coherent understanding across modalities. Understanding these architectures is crucial for appreciating both the capabilities and limitations of current multimodal systems.

Cross-Modal Attention Mechanisms represent one of the most important innovations in multimodal AI. These mechanisms allow systems to focus on relevant information across different modalities while maintaining awareness of the broader context. For example, when analyzing a video of a medical procedure, the system might focus on specific visual elements (surgical instruments, anatomical structures) while simultaneously attending to relevant audio cues (equipment sounds, verbal instructions) and textual information (patient records, procedure protocols).

Fusion Strategies determine how information from different modalities is combined to create unified understanding. Early fusion approaches combine raw data from different sources before processing, while late fusion approaches process each modality separately and then combine the results. Advanced systems employ dynamic fusion strategies that adapt their approach based on the specific task and available data.

Shared Representation Learning enables systems to develop common understanding frameworks that work across multiple modalities. These representations capture abstract concepts and relationships that exist independently of the specific data format, allowing systems to transfer knowledge between modalities and handle novel combinations of data types.

Temporal Alignment mechanisms ensure that information from different modalities is properly synchronized, particularly important for time-series data like video and audio. These mechanisms can handle situations where different data sources have different sampling rates, delays, or temporal structures.

Cross-Modal Translation capabilities allow systems to convert information from one modality to another, such as generating textual descriptions of images or creating visual representations of textual concepts. These capabilities enable systems to fill in missing information and provide outputs in the most appropriate format for specific applications.

Real-World Applications: Multimodal AI in Action

The practical applications of multimodal AI span virtually every industry and domain, with implementations that demonstrate the technology's transformative potential across diverse use cases.

Healthcare Transformation

The Mayo Clinic has implemented multimodal AI systems that revolutionize medical diagnosis and treatment planning. Their diagnostic systems simultaneously analyze medical images (X-rays, MRIs, CT scans), laboratory results, patient symptoms described in natural language, vital signs from monitoring equipment, and historical medical records to provide comprehensive diagnostic assessments.

In radiology, these systems have achieved diagnostic accuracy rates of 94.5% for detecting lung cancer, compared to 87.2% for human radiologists working alone. The improvement comes from the system's ability to correlate subtle visual patterns in imaging data with patient symptoms, medical history, and laboratory results that human radiologists might not immediately connect.

Surgical planning applications use multimodal AI to analyze pre-operative imaging, patient medical history, and real-time surgical video to provide guidance during complex procedures. These systems can identify anatomical structures, predict potential complications, and suggest optimal surgical approaches based on analysis of thousands of similar procedures.

Mental health applications combine analysis of speech patterns, facial expressions, text communications, and physiological data to identify early signs of depression, anxiety, and other mental health conditions. These systems can detect subtle changes that might not be apparent to human observers, enabling earlier intervention and more personalized treatment approaches.

Autonomous Vehicle Intelligence

Tesla's Full Self-Driving system represents one of the most sophisticated implementations of multimodal AI in consumer applications. The system simultaneously processes data from multiple cameras, radar sensors, ultrasonic sensors, and GPS systems to create a comprehensive understanding of the driving environment.

The visual processing component analyzes camera feeds to identify vehicles, pedestrians, traffic signs, road markings, and obstacles. The radar and ultrasonic sensors provide distance and velocity information that complements the visual data. GPS and mapping data provide context about road layouts, traffic patterns, and navigation requirements.

The integration of these data sources enables capabilities that exceed what any single sensor could provide. For example, the system can detect a pedestrian partially obscured by a parked car by combining visual cues from multiple camera angles with radar data indicating movement. It can anticipate traffic light changes by analyzing both the visual appearance of the light and temporal patterns learned from previous experiences at the same intersection.

The results are impressive: Tesla vehicles equipped with Full Self-Driving capability have achieved accident rates 87% lower than the average human driver. This improvement demonstrates the safety benefits of multimodal perception systems that never get tired, distracted, or impaired.

Content Creation and Media

Adobe's Creative Suite has integrated multimodal AI capabilities that transform content creation workflows. Their systems can simultaneously analyze text descriptions, reference images, style preferences, and brand guidelines to generate cohesive visual content that meets specific requirements.

The Photoshop AI features can understand natural language descriptions of desired edits and apply them to images while maintaining visual consistency and quality. For example, a user can request "make the sky more dramatic and add warm lighting" and the system will analyze the existing image, understand the aesthetic intent, and apply appropriate modifications.

Video editing applications use multimodal AI to automatically synchronize audio and visual elements, identify key moments in footage, and generate highlight reels based on content analysis. These systems can recognize emotional expressions, action sequences, and narrative structures to create compelling edited content with minimal human intervention.

Marketing applications analyze brand guidelines, target audience preferences, and campaign objectives to generate coordinated content across multiple channels and formats. These systems ensure consistency in messaging, visual style, and brand representation while adapting content for different platforms and audiences.

Manufacturing and Quality Control

BMW has implemented multimodal AI systems throughout their manufacturing operations to achieve unprecedented levels of quality control and process optimization. These systems simultaneously analyze visual data from high-resolution cameras, audio data from production equipment, sensor data from manufacturing tools, and process data from control systems.

Quality inspection applications can detect defects that would be invisible to human inspectors by correlating subtle visual anomalies with acoustic signatures and process parameters. For example, the system might identify a potential paint defect by analyzing microscopic variations in surface texture, correlating these with spray gun pressure data and environmental conditions during painting.

Predictive maintenance systems analyze vibration patterns, acoustic signatures, thermal imaging data, and operational parameters to predict equipment failures before they occur. These systems have reduced unplanned downtime by 73% while extending equipment life by an average of 18%.

Process optimization applications continuously analyze production data to identify opportunities for improvement. They can detect inefficiencies, recommend parameter adjustments, and predict the impact of changes before implementation. This capability has improved overall equipment effectiveness by 23% while reducing energy consumption by 15%.

The Technical Foundation: Building Multimodal Systems

Implementing multimodal AI systems requires sophisticated technical architectures that can handle the complexity of processing and integrating diverse data types. Understanding these technical requirements is essential for organizations planning multimodal AI implementations.

Data Infrastructure Requirements

Multimodal AI systems require robust data infrastructure capable of handling large volumes of diverse data types with different characteristics and requirements. Visual data requires high-bandwidth storage and processing capabilities, while sensor data may require real-time streaming and low-latency processing.

Data Storage architectures must accommodate different data formats, sizes, and access patterns. Time-series sensor data requires different storage optimization than high-resolution images or unstructured text documents. Modern implementations typically employ hybrid storage architectures that optimize for each data type while maintaining unified access interfaces.

Data Pipeline architectures must handle the ingestion, processing, and synchronization of multiple data streams with different characteristics. Real-time applications require low-latency pipelines that can process and integrate data streams within milliseconds, while batch processing applications can tolerate higher latencies in exchange for more sophisticated analysis.

Data Quality management becomes more complex with multiple data sources that may have different quality characteristics, update frequencies, and reliability levels. Multimodal systems must include robust data validation, cleaning, and quality monitoring capabilities to ensure reliable operation.

Processing Architecture Design

Multimodal AI systems require specialized processing architectures that can efficiently handle the computational demands of simultaneous multi-modal analysis. These architectures must balance processing power, memory requirements, and latency constraints while maintaining scalability and reliability.

Distributed Processing frameworks enable multimodal systems to scale across multiple computing resources while maintaining coordination and consistency. Modern implementations typically employ containerized microservices architectures that can scale individual components based on demand and resource availability.

GPU Acceleration is essential for many multimodal applications, particularly those involving computer vision and deep learning. Modern systems employ specialized GPU clusters optimized for AI workloads, with high-bandwidth interconnects that enable efficient data sharing between processing units.

Edge Computing capabilities are increasingly important for applications requiring real-time processing or operating in environments with limited connectivity. Edge implementations must balance processing capability with power consumption and physical constraints while maintaining integration with cloud-based systems.

Model Architecture and Training

Multimodal AI models require sophisticated architectures that can learn representations and relationships across different data types.

These architectures must handle the different characteristics of various modalities while enabling effective cross-modal learning and inference.

Transformer Architectures have emerged as the dominant approach for many multimodal applications, providing flexible attention mechanisms that can handle variable-length sequences and cross-modal relationships. These architectures can be adapted for different combinations of modalities while maintaining consistent performance characteristics.

Pre-training Strategies for multimodal models typically involve large-scale training on diverse datasets that include multiple modalities. These strategies enable models to learn general representations and relationships that can be fine-tuned for specific applications and domains.

Transfer Learning approaches allow organizations to leverage pre-trained multimodal models and adapt them for specific use cases without requiring massive training datasets or computational resources. This capability significantly reduces the barriers to implementing multimodal AI systems.

Implementation Strategies: Building Multimodal Capabilities

Successfully implementing multimodal AI requires careful planning and systematic execution that addresses both technical and organizational challenges. Organizations that achieve the best results follow proven methodologies that build capabilities incrementally while demonstrating value early in the process.

Phase 1: Foundation and Assessment

The first phase of multimodal AI implementation involves assessing current capabilities, identifying opportunities, and building the foundational infrastructure necessary for multimodal systems.

Data Audit and Mapping involves cataloging all available data sources, understanding their characteristics and quality, and identifying opportunities for multimodal integration. Organizations often discover valuable data sources that were previously underutilized or isolated in departmental silos.

Infrastructure Assessment evaluates current technical capabilities and identifies gaps that must be addressed to support multimodal AI systems. This includes storage capacity, processing power, network bandwidth, and integration capabilities.

Use Case Identification focuses on finding applications where multimodal AI can provide significant value over single-modal approaches. The best initial use cases typically involve well-defined problems with clear success metrics and available data across multiple modalities.

Team Building involves assembling the technical expertise necessary for multimodal AI implementation. This typically includes data scientists with multimodal experience, machine learning engineers, data engineers, and domain experts who understand the specific application areas.

Phase 2: Pilot Implementation

The second phase involves implementing multimodal AI for specific use cases to validate the approach, demonstrate value, and build organizational confidence in the technology.

Pilot Selection should focus on use cases with high business impact, manageable complexity, and clear success criteria. Early wins build momentum and support for broader implementation while providing valuable learning experiences.

Data Integration involves connecting and synchronizing data sources to enable multimodal analysis. This often requires developing new data pipelines, APIs, and integration interfaces that can handle the specific requirements of multimodal systems.

Model Development includes selecting appropriate architectures, training or fine-tuning models for specific use cases, and validating performance across different modalities. Organizations may choose to build custom models, adapt pre-trained models, or use cloud-based multimodal AI services.

Testing and Validation ensures that multimodal systems perform correctly and reliably before full deployment. This includes functional testing across all modalities, performance testing under realistic workloads, and safety testing to ensure robust operation.

Phase 3: Scaling and Optimization

The third phase involves expanding multimodal AI capabilities across the organization and optimizing performance based on operational experience.

Scaling Strategy should prioritize use cases based on business value, technical feasibility, and organizational readiness. Organizations typically scale by expanding successful pilots, implementing multimodal AI for related use cases, or developing more sophisticated multimodal capabilities.

Performance Optimization involves tuning systems for efficiency, accuracy, and reliability based on operational data and user feedback. This includes optimizing model architectures, improving data pipelines, and enhancing integration interfaces.

Continuous Learning mechanisms enable multimodal systems to improve over time through experience and feedback. This includes updating models with new data, refining fusion strategies, and expanding capabilities based on emerging requirements.

Governance and Monitoring ensure that multimodal systems operate safely, ethically, and in compliance with organizational policies and regulatory requirements. This includes establishing monitoring procedures, defining quality metrics, and maintaining human oversight of critical decisions.

Challenges and Considerations: Navigating Multimodal Complexity

While multimodal AI offers tremendous potential, its implementation also presents unique challenges that organizations must address thoughtfully and systematically. Understanding these challenges and developing appropriate mitigation strategies is essential for successful multimodal AI deployment.

Technical Challenges

Data Synchronization represents one of the most significant technical challenges in multimodal AI implementation. Different data sources often have different sampling rates, update frequencies, and temporal characteristics that must be aligned for effective analysis. Video data might be captured at 30 frames per second, while sensor data might be sampled at 1000 Hz, and text data might be updated irregularly based on user input.

Computational Complexity increases significantly with multimodal systems compared to single-modal approaches. Processing multiple data streams simultaneously requires substantial computational resources, and the complexity grows exponentially with the number of modalities and the sophistication of the integration approaches.

Model Complexity and Training multimodal AI models is significantly more challenging than training single-modal models. The models must learn representations and relationships across different data types, which requires larger datasets, more sophisticated architectures, and longer training times.

Integration Challenges arise when connecting multimodal AI systems with existing infrastructure and applications. Legacy systems may not be designed to handle multiple data types or provide the APIs necessary for multimodal integration.

Data Quality and Availability

Multimodal systems are only as good as their weakest data source, and ensuring consistent quality across multiple modalities can be challenging. Different data sources may have different quality characteristics, update frequencies, and reliability levels that can affect overall system performance.

Missing Modality handling becomes critical when one or more data sources are unavailable or unreliable. Multimodal systems must be designed to gracefully degrade performance when some modalities are missing rather than failing completely.

Privacy and Security considerations become more complex with multiple data sources that may have different sensitivity levels and regulatory requirements. Organizations must ensure that multimodal systems comply with all applicable privacy and security regulations while maintaining operational effectiveness.

Organizational Challenges

Skills and Expertise requirements for multimodal AI are more demanding than for single-modal systems. Organizations need team members who understand multiple AI domains, data integration techniques, and the specific challenges of multimodal system design and implementation.

Change Management becomes more complex when multimodal systems affect multiple business processes and stakeholder groups. Different departments may have different perspectives on data sharing, system integration, and workflow changes.

Cost and Resource allocation for multimodal AI projects can be substantial, requiring investments in infrastructure, expertise, and ongoing operational support. Organizations must carefully evaluate the business case and ensure adequate resource allocation for successful implementation.

The Future of Multimodal AI: Emerging Trends and Capabilities

The field of multimodal AI is evolving rapidly, with new capabilities and applications emerging continuously. Understanding these trends is essential for organizations planning long-term multimodal AI strategies and preparing for future opportunities.

Advanced Integration Techniques

Next-generation multimodal systems are developing increasingly sophisticated integration techniques that enable more seamless and effective combination of different data types. These techniques go beyond simple concatenation or parallel processing to create truly integrated understanding across modalities.

Neural Architecture Search is being applied to automatically discover optimal multimodal architectures for specific applications and data combinations. These techniques can identify novel integration approaches that human designers might not consider while optimizing for specific performance criteria.

Dynamic Fusion strategies adapt their integration approach based on the specific data available and the task requirements. These systems can automatically adjust their processing based on data quality, availability, and relevance to provide optimal performance under varying conditions.

Cross-Modal Generation capabilities enable systems to create content in one modality based on input from another modality. For example, generating realistic images from text descriptions or creating audio narrations from visual content.

Real-Time Multimodal Processing

The demand for real-time multimodal AI is driving innovations in processing efficiency and system architecture. These developments enable applications that require immediate response to multimodal inputs, such as autonomous vehicles, robotics, and interactive systems.

Edge Multimodal AI brings sophisticated multimodal processing capabilities to edge devices, enabling real-time analysis without dependence on cloud connectivity. These systems must balance processing capability with power consumption and physical constraints.

Streaming Multimodal Analysis enables continuous processing of multimodal data streams with minimal latency. These systems can handle high-volume, high-velocity data while maintaining accuracy and reliability.

Adaptive Processing techniques adjust computational resource allocation based on the complexity and importance of different data streams and analysis tasks. These approaches optimize performance while managing resource constraints.

Emerging Application Domains

New application domains for multimodal AI are emerging as the technology matures and becomes more accessible. These applications demonstrate the expanding potential of multimodal approaches across diverse industries and use cases.

Augmented Reality applications use multimodal AI to understand and interact with the physical world through multiple sensors and data sources. These systems can overlay digital information on physical environments while understanding context and user intent.

Smart City applications integrate data from multiple sources including traffic cameras, environmental sensors, social media, and mobile devices to optimize urban operations and services. These systems can improve traffic flow, reduce energy consumption, and enhance public safety.

Personalized Education systems use multimodal AI to understand individual learning styles, preferences, and progress through analysis of multiple data sources including text responses, video interactions, and physiological indicators.

Embracing Multimodal Intelligence

Multimodal AI represents a fundamental shift in how machines understand and interact with the world. By breaking down the artificial barriers between different types of data and creating systems that can integrate information across modalities, we are moving closer to AI systems that can understand the world as richly and comprehensively as humans do.

The applications and benefits of multimodal AI are already evident across industries, from healthcare and autonomous vehicles to manufacturing and content creation. Organizations that successfully implement multimodal AI capabilities are achieving significant competitive advantages through improved accuracy, efficiency, and capability.

However, realizing the full potential of multimodal AI requires more than simply combining different AI technologies. It requires thoughtful system design, careful attention to data quality and integration, and systematic approaches to implementation and scaling. Organizations must also address the unique challenges of multimodal systems, including increased complexity, higher resource requirements, and more sophisticated governance needs.

The future of multimodal AI is bright, with emerging capabilities that will enable even more sophisticated applications and use cases. Organizations that invest in building multimodal AI capabilities today will be well-positioned to take advantage of these future developments and maintain competitive advantages in an increasingly AI-driven economy.

The choice is clear: embrace multimodal AI and unlock the potential of integrated intelligence, or risk being left behind by organizations that do. The technology is ready, the applications are proven, and the benefits are substantial for those bold enough to pursue them.

In the next chapter, we explore what happens when machines don't just perceive—but create. When intelligence becomes generative.

What does it mean for a machine to write, paint, compose, or invent?

And how do we navigate the line between inspiration and imitation?

Let's continue.

Chapter 3
Generative AI

The Creative Force Driving Innovation

> "We taught the machine to learn. Now it's learning to create."
> — MIT Computational Creativity Lab, 2023

3.1 The Rise of Synthetic Creativity

For most of history, creativity was considered uniquely human. It was the domain of poets, artists, designers, and inventors—the ones who imagined what didn't yet exist. But in recent years, that assumption has been disrupted.

Generative AI refers to artificial intelligence systems capable of producing original content—text, images, music, code, video, simulations, and even physical design blueprints. These systems don't simply remix existing material. They generate new patterns, new expressions, and increasingly, new possibilities.

What began as quirky experiments—machines writing haiku or sketching cats—has now become a mainstream engine of productivity and innovation.

3.2 What Powers Generative AI?

At the heart of this revolution are foundation models—massive neural networks trained on vast datasets that learn the structures and syntax of language, imagery, and behavior.

Three primary types of generative systems include:

- Large Language Models (LLMs) – Trained on billions of words, these models can draft essays, summarize reports, write code, answer questions, and hold conversations with startling fluency.

- Generative Adversarial Networks (GANs) – Involving two models—a generator and a discriminator—that compete to produce increasingly realistic outputs, such as photorealistic portraits, architectural mockups, or clothing designs.

- Diffusion Models – Newer models that generate images by gradually refining random noise into detailed visuals.

  Think of it like a sculptor starting with a block of static and chiseling away until a coherent image emerges.

Together, these models form the core of a new kind of creative engine—neither fully human nor purely algorithmic, but something in between.

3.3 Applications Across Industries

3.3.1

Marketing and Branding

- Generative tools can produce dozens of ad variations, slogans, and visuals tailored to specific demographics.

- AI platforms like Jasper and Copy.ai are used across industries to scale content creation without losing tone or coherence.

3.3.2

Entertainment and Storytelling

- Filmmakers use AI to pre-visualize scenes, generate storyboards, and simulate lighting and set design—cutting weeks off production timelines.

- Virtual influencers like Lil Miquela, created entirely through generative systems, now secure brand sponsorships and dominate digital platforms.

3.3.3

Product Design and Prototyping

- Architects and engineers input constraints and let AI generate optimized models.

- Automotive and aerospace companies use generative systems to evolve vehicle parts that maximize performance and reduce material waste.

3.3.4

Scientific Research and Discovery

- Protein folding models like AlphaFold use generative techniques to accelerate drug development by simulating biological structures in minutes.

3.3.5

Education and Personalized Learning

- Adaptive tutoring systems generate customized content, quizzes, and lesson sequences in real time—responding to learner performance and engagement.

3.4 Generative vs. Human Creativity

While generative AI can produce stunning results, the question persists: Is it truly creative?

Human creativity is often grounded in emotion, memory, intent, and cultural resonance. Generative systems, by contrast, operate statistically—predicting what is likely to come next in a given context.

Still, the gap is narrowing:

- AI-generated paintings sell at auction.
- AI-assisted songs chart on streaming platforms.
- AI-written poetry appears in literary journals—occasionally without disclosure.

Rather than replacing artists, many professionals now collaborate with AI systems.

Example: In Hollywood, directors use AI-powered visualization tools to rapidly prototype scenes—experimenting with camera angles, color grading, and lighting before stepping onto set. These tools don't replace cinematographers—they extend their reach.

3.5 Ethical Implications and Intellectual Property

Authorship and Ownership

Who owns AI-generated content? Is it the person who wrote the prompt? The developers of the model? The platform hosting the system?

Legal frameworks around copyright and authorship are still evolving, with test cases emerging in music, publishing, and design.

Deepfakes and Disinformation

AI can now generate convincing video and audio impersonations of real people.

Example: In 2023, a deepfake video of Ukrainian President Volodymyr Zelensky appearing to surrender circulated widely—causing confusion and diplomatic alarm before it was debunked.

Cultural Appropriation and Style Theft

Artists have protested the scraping of their works to train models without consent.

Some have turned to tools like Glaze, which subtly distorts artwork in ways invisible to humans but disruptive to AI scrapers—an act of digital self-defense.

3.6 Reframing the Creative Process

Rather than viewing generative AI as a replacement for human imagination, many creators now treat it as an amplifier—an intelligent co-creator that expands the realm of what's possible.

- Writers use LLMs to explore alternative phrasing, tone, or plot structure.

- Musicians remix AI-generated melodies into compositions that blend machine logic with human emotion.

- Designers use AI to brainstorm hundreds of ideas—then refine the best into final products.

In this new paradigm, creativity is no longer about control. It's about curation, synthesis, and collaboration.

3.7 Human Futures in a Generative World

Generative AI invites wonder—but also deep reflection.

When machines can produce at scale, originality becomes more valuable. When imitation is easy, intention matters more.

We must ask:

What defines authenticity in a world of infinite generation?

How do we ensure diversity, ethics, and nuance in systems that can simulate any style?

And perhaps most importantly:

Can a machine truly capture the ache of a breakup song or the defiance of a protest painting?

As AI enters the studio, the writer's room, the classroom, and the laboratory, our task is not to resist its presence—but to shape its purpose.

Generative AI - The New Renaissance of Creation

"We are witnessing the democratization of creativity itself—a moment when the power to create, design, and innovate is no longer limited by technical skill or resource constraints, but only by the boundaries of human imagination."

In a converted warehouse in Brooklyn, Maya Chen sits before her computer screen, watching in amazement as her ideas transform into reality with unprecedented speed and sophistication. As a freelance graphic designer, she once spent weeks creating marketing campaigns for clients, painstakingly crafting each element by hand. Today, she describes her vision in natural language to an AI system that generates dozens of design variations in minutes, each professionally crafted and ready for refinement.

"Create a luxury brand identity for a sustainable fashion company targeting millennials," she types. "The aesthetic should be minimalist but warm, incorporating earth tones and organic shapes. Include logo variations, business cards, packaging design, and social media templates." Within three minutes, the AI presents her with a comprehensive brand package that would have taken her team weeks to produce manually.

But Maya's story represents just one facet of a much larger transformation. Across the globe, generative AI is revolutionizing how humans create, design, and innovate. Writers are collaborating with AI to produce novels, screenplays, and marketing copy. Musicians are composing symphonies with AI partners that understand harmony, rhythm, and emotional expression. Architects are designing buildings with AI systems that optimize for aesthetics, functionality, and sustainability simultaneously. Software developers are building applications with AI assistants that can write, debug, and optimize code faster than any human programmer.

This is the generative AI revolution—a transformation so profound that it is reshaping the very nature of creative work and intellectual production.

Understanding Generative AI: The Technology of Creation

Generative AI represents a fundamental shift from AI systems that analyze and classify existing information to systems that create entirely new content. These systems can produce text, images, audio, video, code, and even complex designs that are original, coherent, and often indistinguishable from human-created content.

The technology builds upon decades of research in machine learning, neural networks, and natural language processing, but recent breakthroughs in transformer architectures, diffusion models, and large-scale training have created capabilities that seemed impossible just a few years ago. The global generative AI market, valued at $13.7 billion in 2023, is projected to reach $255.8 billion by 2033, representing a compound annual growth rate of 34.2%.

What makes generative AI truly revolutionary is not just its ability to create content, but its capacity to understand context, style, and intent in ways that enable meaningful collaboration with humans. These systems don't simply recombine existing elements—they demonstrate genuine creativity, producing novel solutions and unexpected insights that can inspire and enhance human creativity.

The impact extends far beyond individual productivity gains. Generative AI is democratizing access to sophisticated creative tools, enabling small businesses to compete with large corporations, allowing individuals to express ideas that were previously beyond their technical capabilities, and accelerating innovation across industries by reducing the time and cost of experimentation and iteration.

The Architecture of Creativity: How Generative AI Works

Understanding the technical foundations of generative AI is essential for appreciating both its capabilities and limitations. Modern generative AI systems employ sophisticated architectures that enable them to learn patterns from vast datasets and use those patterns to create new, original content.

Large Language Models (LLMs) form the foundation of many generative AI systems. These models are trained on massive text datasets, learning the statistical patterns of language, knowledge, and reasoning. Advanced LLMs like GPT-4, Claude, and Gemini contain hundreds of billions of parameters that encode understanding of grammar, facts, concepts, and relationships.

The training process involves exposing these models to enormous amounts of text from books, articles, websites, and other sources, allowing them to learn how language works at multiple levels—from basic grammar and syntax to complex reasoning and creative expression. The result is systems that can generate coherent, contextually appropriate text on virtually any topic.

Diffusion Models have revolutionized image generation by learning to gradually transform random noise into coherent images. These models are trained on millions of image-text pairs, learning to associate visual concepts with textual descriptions. During generation, they start with random noise and iteratively refine it based on text prompts, creating images that match the specified description.

The sophistication of modern diffusion models like DALL-E 3, Midjourney, and Stable Diffusion enables them to create images with remarkable detail, artistic style, and conceptual coherence. They can understand complex prompts involving multiple objects, specific artistic styles, lighting conditions, and compositional elements.

Transformer Architectures provide the underlying framework for many generative AI systems. These architectures use attention mechanisms that allow models to focus on relevant parts of their input when generating each part of their output. This capability enables them to maintain coherence across long sequences and understand complex relationships between different elements.

The attention mechanism is particularly important for creative tasks because it allows models to consider multiple factors simultaneously—style, content, context, and constraints—while generating new content. This capability enables the sophisticated creative reasoning that makes generative AI so powerful.

Multimodal Integration in advanced generative systems enables them to work across different types of content simultaneously. These systems can generate images from text descriptions, create text from images, or even produce videos that combine visual and audio elements based on textual instructions.

This multimodal capability is particularly powerful for creative applications because it mirrors how humans think about creative projects—considering visual, textual, and conceptual elements together rather than in isolation.

Real-World Applications: Generative AI Transforming Industries

The practical applications of generative AI span virtually every industry and creative domain, with implementations that demonstrate the technology's transformative potential across diverse use cases.

Content Creation and Marketing Revolution

Jasper AI has transformed content marketing for over 100,000 businesses worldwide, enabling them to produce high-quality marketing content at unprecedented scale and speed. Companies using Jasper report average productivity improvements of 125% in content creation, with some achieving output increases of over 300% while maintaining quality standards.

Coca-Cola has implemented generative AI across their global marketing operations, using the technology to create personalized advertisements, social media content, and campaign materials for different markets and demographics. The system can generate culturally appropriate content in dozens of languages while maintaining brand consistency and messaging coherence.

The results have been remarkable: campaign development time has decreased from months to weeks, personalization capabilities have improved dramatically, and marketing ROI has increased by an average of 23% across markets. The technology enables Coca-Cola to test hundreds of creative variations quickly and cost-effectively, identifying the most effective approaches before committing to large-scale production.

Netflix uses generative AI to create personalized artwork for their content library, generating thousands of variations of movie and show thumbnails tailored to individual user preferences and viewing history. The system analyzes user behavior, content preferences, and engagement patterns to create artwork that maximizes click-through rates and viewing engagement.

This personalization extends beyond simple image generation to include trailer creation, content descriptions, and even recommendation explanations. The result has been a 18% increase in content engagement and a 12% improvement in user retention rates.

Software Development Transformation

GitHub Copilot has revolutionized software development by providing AI-powered code generation and completion capabilities to over 1.3 million developers worldwide. Developers using Copilot report completing tasks 55% faster on average, with some experiencing productivity improvements exceeding 100% for routine coding tasks.

Microsoft's internal studies show that developers using Copilot write code 88% faster, spend 74% less time on repetitive tasks, and report 73% higher job satisfaction due to reduced frustration with routine coding work. The technology enables developers to focus on higher-level problem-solving and creative aspects of software development rather than syntax and boilerplate code.

Replit has integrated generative AI throughout their development platform, enabling users to build complete applications through natural language descriptions. Users can describe the functionality they want, and the AI generates the necessary code, database schemas, user interfaces, and deployment configurations.

The platform has democratized software development, enabling individuals without extensive programming experience to create sophisticated applications. Educational institutions report that students using AI-assisted development tools learn programming concepts 40% faster while building more ambitious projects.

Creative Industries Renaissance

Adobe has integrated generative AI across their Creative Suite, transforming workflows for millions of creative professionals worldwide. Photoshop's generative fill feature enables users to add, remove, or modify image elements through natural language descriptions, while Illustrator's AI tools can generate vector graphics and design elements based on text prompts.

Professional designers report that AI-assisted workflows reduce project completion time by 30-50% while enabling them to explore more creative variations and possibilities. The technology doesn't replace human creativity but amplifies it, allowing designers to iterate faster and experiment with ideas that would be too time-consuming to explore manually.

Runway ML has pioneered AI-powered video generation and editing tools that are transforming film and video production. Their systems can generate video content from text descriptions, extend existing footage, and apply sophisticated visual effects that previously required expensive specialized software and extensive technical expertise.

Independent filmmakers and content creators report that AI-powered video tools have reduced production costs by 60-80% while enabling creative possibilities that were previously beyond their reach. The democratization of sophisticated video production tools is creating new opportunities for storytelling and creative expression.

Scientific Research and Discovery

DeepMind's AlphaFold has revolutionized protein structure prediction, generating accurate 3D models of protein structures that would take years to determine experimentally. The system has predicted structures for over 200 million proteins, accelerating drug discovery and biological research across the globe.

Pharmaceutical companies using AlphaFold predictions report 25-40% reductions in early-stage drug discovery timelines, with some achieving breakthrough insights that would have been impossible through traditional experimental approaches alone. The technology has enabled new approaches to treating diseases and understanding biological processes.

Anthropic's Claude has been used by researchers to generate hypotheses, analyze complex datasets, and even write research papers in collaboration with human scientists. The AI can process vast amounts of scientific literature, identify patterns and connections that humans might miss, and suggest novel research directions and experimental approaches.

Research teams using AI assistance report 35% faster literature reviews, 28% more comprehensive hypothesis generation, and 22% higher success rates in grant applications due to more thorough and innovative research proposals.

The Economics of Generative AI: Measuring the Impact

The economic impact of generative AI is both measurable and substantial, with organizations across industries reporting significant improvements in productivity, cost reduction, and revenue generation. Understanding these economic effects is crucial for organizations planning generative AI investments and strategies.

Productivity and Efficiency Gains

A comprehensive study by McKinsey found that organizations implementing generative AI achieve average productivity improvements of 20-25% across affected business functions. These improvements stem from several factors: faster content creation, reduced time spent on routine tasks, improved quality and consistency, and enhanced creative capabilities.

The consulting industry has seen particularly dramatic results. Boston Consulting Group reports that consultants using generative AI complete projects 25% faster while producing higher-quality deliverables. The technology enables consultants to rapidly generate analysis frameworks, create presentation materials, and develop recommendations based on comprehensive data analysis.

Legal services have experienced similar transformations. Law firms using AI-powered document generation and analysis tools report 40-60% reductions in time spent on routine legal work, enabling lawyers to focus on higher-value strategic and advisory activities. Client satisfaction has improved due to faster turnaround times and more comprehensive analysis.

Cost Reduction and Resource Optimization

Generative AI enables organizations to achieve significant cost reductions through automation of content creation, reduced need for specialized expertise, and improved resource utilization. A study by Accenture found that companies implementing generative AI achieve average cost reductions of 15-30% in affected business processes.

Marketing departments report particularly substantial savings. Companies using AI-generated content achieve 50-70% reductions in content creation costs while producing 3-5 times more content variations for testing and optimization. This capability enables more sophisticated marketing strategies that were previously cost-prohibitive.

Training and education organizations report 40-60% cost reductions in content development through AI-assisted course creation, while achieving better learning outcomes through personalized content generation. The technology enables rapid development of training materials tailored to specific audiences and learning objectives.

Revenue Generation and Business Model Innovation

Generative AI is not just reducing costs—it's enabling new revenue streams and business models that were previously impossible. Companies are using AI-generated content to create personalized products, develop new services, and enter markets that were previously inaccessible.

Shutterstock has built a thriving business around AI-generated stock imagery, offering customers unlimited access to custom-generated images for a fraction of the cost of traditional stock photography. The service has attracted over 500,000 users and generated millions in new revenue while expanding the market for visual content.

Educational technology companies are using generative AI to create personalized learning experiences that adapt to individual student needs and learning styles. These AI-powered educational platforms achieve 40% better learning outcomes while reducing per-student costs by 25%.

Implementation Strategies: Building Generative AI Capabilities

Successfully implementing generative AI requires careful planning, strategic thinking, and systematic execution that addresses both technical and organizational challenges. Organizations that achieve the best results follow proven methodologies that build capabilities incrementally while demonstrating value early in the process.

Phase 1: Strategy and Foundation Building

The first phase of generative AI implementation involves developing a clear strategy, assessing organizational readiness, and building the foundational capabilities necessary for successful deployment.

Strategic Planning begins with identifying use cases where generative AI can provide significant value over traditional approaches. The best initial use cases typically involve content creation tasks that are time-consuming, require consistency, or benefit from rapid iteration and experimentation.

Content Audit and Analysis involves cataloging existing content creation processes, identifying bottlenecks and inefficiencies, and determining where AI generation can provide the most impact. Organizations often discover opportunities for AI assistance in areas they hadn't previously considered.

Quality Standards Development is crucial for ensuring that AI-generated content meets organizational requirements for accuracy, brand consistency, and appropriateness. This includes developing evaluation criteria, review processes, and quality control mechanisms.

Team Preparation involves training staff on generative AI capabilities, limitations, and best practices. Successful implementations require team members who understand how to work effectively with AI tools while maintaining quality and oversight.

Phase 2: Pilot Implementation and Learning

The second phase involves implementing generative AI for specific use cases to validate the approach, demonstrate value, and build organizational confidence in the technology.

Pilot Selection should focus on use cases with clear success metrics, manageable scope, and high potential impact. Early wins build momentum and support for broader implementation while providing valuable learning experiences about effective AI integration.

Tool Selection and Integration involves choosing appropriate generative AI platforms and integrating them with existing workflows and systems. Organizations may choose to use cloud-based services, develop custom solutions, or implement hybrid approaches based on their specific requirements.

Workflow Design requires reimagining content creation processes to effectively incorporate AI generation while maintaining quality control and human oversight. This often involves developing new review processes, approval workflows, and collaboration patterns.

Performance Measurement establishes metrics for evaluating the success of generative AI implementations. Key metrics typically include productivity improvements, quality measures, cost savings, and user satisfaction scores.

Phase 3: Scaling and Optimization

The third phase involves expanding generative AI capabilities across the organization and optimizing performance based on operational experience and feedback.

Scaling Strategy should prioritize use cases based on business value, technical feasibility, and organizational readiness. Organizations typically scale by expanding successful pilots, implementing AI generation for related use cases, or developing more sophisticated AI capabilities.

Process Optimization involves refining workflows, improving prompt engineering techniques, and enhancing integration with existing systems based on operational experience. This includes developing templates, standardizing approaches, and automating routine tasks.

Advanced Capabilities Development may include custom model training, fine-tuning for specific domains, or developing specialized AI tools for unique organizational requirements. These advanced capabilities can provide competitive advantages and address specific business needs.

Governance and Quality Assurance become increasingly important as generative AI usage scales across the organization. This includes establishing monitoring procedures, maintaining quality standards, and ensuring compliance with legal and ethical requirements.

Challenges and Considerations: Navigating Generative AI Complexity

While generative AI offers tremendous potential, its implementation also presents unique challenges that organizations must address thoughtfully and systematically. Understanding these challenges and developing appropriate mitigation strategies is essential for successful generative AI deployment.

Quality and Reliability Challenges

Content Quality Variability represents one of the most significant challenges in generative AI implementation. While AI systems can produce high-quality content, they can also generate outputs that are inaccurate, inappropriate, or inconsistent with organizational standards. Ensuring consistent quality requires robust review processes and quality control mechanisms.

Hallucination and Accuracy Issues occur when AI systems generate plausible-sounding but factually incorrect information. This is particularly problematic for applications requiring high accuracy, such as technical documentation, legal content, or medical information. Organizations must implement fact-checking processes and verification procedures.

Brand Consistency and Voice maintenance becomes challenging when multiple team members use AI tools with different prompting approaches and quality standards. Organizations need clear guidelines, templates, and review processes to ensure consistent brand representation across AI-generated content.

Intellectual Property and Legal Considerations

Copyright and Ownership questions arise when AI systems generate content based on training data that may include copyrighted material. Organizations must understand the legal implications of using AI-generated content and ensure compliance with intellectual property laws.

Attribution and Transparency requirements are evolving as regulators and industry groups develop guidelines for AI-generated content. Organizations may need to disclose when content is

AI-generated and ensure appropriate attribution for human contributions.

Liability and Responsibility issues become complex when AI-generated content causes harm or violates regulations. Organizations need clear policies for accountability and liability when using AI-generated content in their operations.

Ethical and Social Considerations

Bias and Fairness concerns arise when AI systems perpetuate or amplify biases present in their training data. This can result in generated content that reflects stereotypes, excludes certain groups, or promotes unfair representations. Organizations must implement bias detection and mitigation strategies.

Job Displacement Concerns affect employees whose roles involve content creation tasks that may be automated through generative AI. Organizations need thoughtful change management strategies that help employees adapt to new roles and responsibilities.

Authenticity and Human Value questions emerge as AI-generated content becomes more sophisticated and prevalent. Organizations must consider how to maintain human creativity and authentic expression while leveraging AI capabilities.

The Future of Generative AI: Emerging Trends and Capabilities

The field of generative AI is evolving rapidly, with new capabilities and applications emerging continuously. Understanding these trends is essential for organizations planning long-term generative AI strategies and preparing for future opportunities.

Advanced Multimodal Generation

Next-generation generative AI systems are developing increasingly sophisticated capabilities for creating content across multiple modalities simultaneously. These systems can generate coordinated text, images, audio, and video content that maintains consistency and coherence across different formats.

Video Generation capabilities are advancing rapidly, with systems like Sora demonstrating the ability to create high-quality video content from text descriptions [58]. These capabilities will enable new forms of content creation and storytelling that were previously impossible or prohibitively expensive.

Interactive Content Generation enables AI systems to create dynamic, responsive content that adapts to user interactions and preferences in real-time. This capability will enable new forms of personalized experiences and interactive media.

Specialized Domain Applications

Industry-Specific Models are being developed for specialized domains like legal, medical, financial, and scientific applications. These models are trained on domain-specific data and optimized for the unique requirements and constraints of particular industries.

Code Generation capabilities are becoming increasingly sophisticated, with systems that can generate complete applications, debug existing code, and optimize performance based on natural language descriptions of requirements.

Scientific Discovery applications use generative AI to propose new hypotheses, design experiments, and even generate novel molecular structures for drug discovery and materials science applications.

Enhanced Human-AI Collaboration

Collaborative Creation tools are evolving to enable more seamless integration between human creativity and AI generation. These tools understand human intent, maintain creative consistency, and adapt to individual working styles and preferences.

Real-Time Assistance capabilities enable AI systems to provide suggestions, corrections, and enhancements as humans work, creating more fluid and natural collaboration experiences.

Personalized AI Assistants learn individual preferences, styles, and requirements to provide increasingly tailored and effective assistance for creative and content creation tasks.

Embracing the Creative Revolution

Generative AI represents one of the most transformative technologies of our time, with the potential to democratize creativity, accelerate innovation, and enable new forms of human expression and productivity. The technology is not just automating existing creative processes—it is expanding the very definition of what is possible in creative and intellectual work.

Organizations that successfully implement generative AI capabilities are achieving significant competitive advantages through improved productivity, reduced costs, and enhanced creative capabilities. The technology enables small teams to compete with large organizations, individuals to express ideas that were previously beyond their technical capabilities, and businesses to experiment and innovate at unprecedented speed and scale.

However, realizing the full potential of generative AI requires more than simply adopting new tools. It requires thoughtful planning, systematic implementation, and ongoing adaptation to changing capabilities and requirements. Organizations must address quality and reliability challenges, navigate legal and ethical considerations, and develop new workflows and governance approaches.

The future of generative AI is bright, with emerging capabilities that will enable even more sophisticated applications and use cases. Organizations that invest in building generative AI capabilities today will be well-positioned to take advantage of these future developments and maintain competitive advantages in an increasingly AI-driven economy.

The creative revolution is underway, and the opportunities are unprecedented for those bold enough to embrace them. The choice is clear: harness the power of generative AI to unlock human creative potential, or risk being left behind by organizations that do. The technology is ready, the applications are proven, and the benefits are substantial for those who choose to lead rather than follow.

Looking Ahead

Generative AI marks a turning point—not just in what machines can do, but in what we choose to do with them.

The next chapter turns from creation to location—exploring how intelligence is migrating from massive cloud servers into the physical world around us.

When AI is embedded directly into our phones, homes, factories, and vehicles, how does it change?

Let's explore Edge AI—the quiet revolution happening right in your hands.

Chapter 4
Edge AI

Intelligence at the Device Level

> "The next generation of AI won't live in the cloud.
> It will live in your pocket, your car, your city."
>
> — Intel Edge Computing Initiative, 2024

4.1 What Is Edge AI?

For years, AI systems have been synonymous with the cloud—data collected on your phone is processed in distant servers, and responses are sent back over a network. But what happens when the cloud isn't fast enough, private enough, or available at all?

Edge AI is the solution.

Edge AI refers to artificial intelligence algorithms that run directly on local hardware—on smartphones, IoT devices, drones, vehicles, sensors, and machines—without depending on constant cloud connectivity. The result? Decisions made faster, privately, and often in real time.

It's not just a technical shift. It's a philosophical one: bringing intelligence closer to where life actually happens.

4.2 Why Edge Matters: Speed, Privacy, and Autonomy

Three reasons explain the rise of edge computing in AI systems:

Latency Reduction

In scenarios like autonomous driving, medical monitoring, or robotics, milliseconds matter.

Cloud-based systems introduce delays; edge AI eliminates the need to wait.

Example: A self-driving car can't afford a 200ms delay while waiting for cloud-based object recognition. Edge systems process camera data locally—braking or steering in under 10 milliseconds.

Data Privacy and Sovereignty

Keeping data on-device means less exposure.

Personal health information, security camera footage, or biometric data can be analyzed locally—without sending anything to external servers.

Reliability in Low-Connectivity Zones

From smart farms to remote industrial sites, edge AI ensures functionality even without stable internet access.

In disaster zones or rural regions, this can be the difference between success and failure.

4.3 Where It's Already Being Used

Edge AI is already transforming everyday technology—often invisibly.

4.3.1 Smartphones

- Your phone's camera uses AI to detect faces, blur backgrounds, and optimize lighting—all on-device.

- Speech recognition and predictive text increasingly operate offline to protect privacy and save bandwidth.

4.3.2 Smart Homes and Cities

- Security systems detect intrusions and analyze motion without relying on cloud servers.

- Smart thermostats learn your preferences locally, adjusting climate control in real time.

4.3.3 Wearables and Health Devices

- Fitness trackers monitor heart rate, sleep patterns, and oxygen levels, triggering alerts without uploading sensitive data.

- AI-powered hearing aids enhance sound based on real-time environmental analysis.

4.3.4 Industrial IoT

- Machines on factory floors run diagnostic algorithms to predict maintenance needs—preventing downtime and saving costs.

- Oil rigs, power plants, and mining equipment rely on rugged edge AI modules that function even in extreme environments.

4.3.5 Transportation and Vehicles

- Drones analyze visual input for navigation and object avoidance locally.
- Modern vehicles use AI to monitor driver alertness, detect hazards, and adjust systems—no data ever leaves the car.

4.4 Under the Hood: How Edge AI Works

Running AI locally requires innovation across both hardware and software.

Model Compression Techniques

To run efficiently on low-power chips, AI models are made smaller and faster using techniques like:

- Quantization – Reducing numerical precision without major loss of accuracy
- Pruning – Removing redundant neurons and pathways
- Knowledge Distillation – Training smaller models to replicate the behavior of larger ones

Think of it like a student learning from a professor's condensed notes—capturing essential wisdom in a compact form.

Specialized Hardware

Edge AI uses chips optimized for inference tasks, such as:

- Neural Processing Units (NPUs)
- Tensor Processing Units (TPUs)
- Vision Processing Units (VPUs) for handling camera data

These allow AI workloads to be run efficiently on phones, microcontrollers, and embedded boards.

4.5 Security, Ethics, and Design Tradeoffs

Security

While data is processed locally, edge devices are still vulnerable. Physical theft, firmware exploits, and remote attacks can compromise on-device systems.

Example: Apple's Secure Enclave protects biometric data by isolating it from the operating system and encrypting it in dedicated hardware—showcasing robust tamper detection in action.

Bias and Accountability

Local models must still be evaluated for bias—especially in high-stakes contexts like surveillance, policing, or healthcare. Lack of transparency or explainability can compound risks if not actively addressed.

Energy Use

Some edge applications (e.g., smart cameras running 24/7) pose energy tradeoffs. Efficient model design and edge-optimized chipsets help mitigate power drain—but conscious energy profiling is essential.

Update Complexity

Cloud models can be updated centrally. Edge models require more complex distribution, testing, and coordination across devices—which can lead to version drift or delayed safety fixes.

4.6 A Hybrid Future: Edge + Cloud

In reality, the future isn't edge versus cloud—it's edge plus cloud.

Hybrid architectures allow for:

- Real-time decision-making on the edge
- Deeper analysis and retraining in the cloud
- Federated learning, where models are trained collaboratively across many devices without exposing personal data

This allows intelligence to be both scalable and personalized—local actions optimized by global patterns.

4.7 Edge AI as a Force for Equity

Perhaps the most transformative power of edge AI lies in accessibility.

- Remote schools can deliver AI-powered learning tools even without broadband.

Example: Raspberry Pi-powered AI tutors are being piloted in rural India, offering offline education tools in local languages.

- Health monitoring in underserved areas becomes possible without centralized infrastructure.

- Privacy-respecting devices allow vulnerable populations to use technology without sacrificing autonomy.

By reducing dependency on centralized systems, edge AI offers a path toward digital equity—intelligence at the edge of the network, in the hands of everyone.

Intelligence Everywhere, Instantly

"The future of AI is not in distant data centers, but in the devices around us—in our phones, our cars, our homes, and our cities. Intelligence is becoming ambient, invisible, and instantaneous."

At 3:47 AM on a foggy Tuesday morning in rural Montana, a combine harvester navigates through a wheat field with precision that would be impossible for any human operator. The machine's edge AI system simultaneously processes data from dozens of sensors—soil moisture readings, crop density measurements, weather conditions, and GPS coordinates—making thousands of micro-adjustments per second to optimize harvesting efficiency while minimizing crop damage.

There is no cellular signal for miles, no connection to cloud servers, no dependency on distant data centers. The intelligence required to make these complex decisions resides entirely within the machine itself, processing information and making decisions in real-time with latency measured in milliseconds rather than seconds.

This scenario illustrates the transformative power of edge AI—artificial intelligence that operates directly on local devices rather than relying on cloud-based processing. This technology is enabling a new era of intelligent systems that can respond instantly to changing conditions, operate reliably in challenging environments, and provide sophisticated capabilities without dependence on network connectivity.

Understanding Edge AI: Intelligence at the Point of Need

Edge AI represents a fundamental shift in how and where artificial intelligence operates. Rather than sending data to distant cloud servers for processing, edge AI brings intelligence directly to the devices and locations where decisions need to be made. This approach offers several critical advantages: dramatically reduced latency, improved privacy and security, reduced bandwidth requirements, and enhanced reliability in environments with limited or unreliable connectivity.

The global edge AI market is experiencing explosive growth, projected to expand from $15.7 billion in 2024 to $83.9 billion by 2030, representing a compound annual growth rate of 32.1%. This growth is driven by the increasing demand for real-time AI capabilities, the proliferation of IoT devices, and the need for AI systems that can operate reliably in diverse and challenging environments.

Edge AI is not simply a deployment strategy—it represents a new paradigm for AI system design that prioritizes efficiency, responsiveness, and autonomy. These systems must operate within strict constraints of power consumption, processing capability, and memory while delivering sophisticated AI capabilities that rival cloud-based systems.

The technology is enabling applications that were previously impossible or impractical, from autonomous vehicles that must make split-second decisions to industrial equipment that operates in environments without reliable connectivity. Edge AI is making artificial intelligence truly ubiquitous, embedding intelligence into every aspect of our physical world.

The Architecture of Distributed Intelligence: How Edge AI Works

Edge AI systems employ specialized architectures designed to deliver sophisticated AI capabilities within the constraints of local devices and environments. Understanding these architectures is essential for appreciating both the capabilities and limitations of edge AI implementations.

Optimized Model Architectures are specifically designed for edge deployment, balancing accuracy with computational efficiency. These models employ techniques like quantization, pruning, and knowledge distillation to reduce model size and computational requirements while maintaining performance.

Quantization reduces the precision of model parameters, typically from 32-bit floating-point numbers to 8-bit or even 4-bit integers. This reduction can decrease model size by 75% or more while maintaining acceptable accuracy levels. Advanced quantization techniques can achieve even greater compression with minimal accuracy loss.

Pruning removes unnecessary connections and parameters from neural networks, creating sparse models that require less computation and memory. Structured pruning can eliminate entire layers or channels, while unstructured pruning removes individual weights based on their importance to model performance.

Knowledge Distillation transfers knowledge from large, complex models to smaller, more efficient models suitable for edge deployment. The smaller "student" models learn to mimic the behavior of larger "teacher" models while requiring significantly fewer computational resources.

Specialized Hardware Acceleration enables edge devices to perform AI computations efficiently despite limited resources. This includes dedicated AI chips, optimized processors, and specialized accelerators designed specifically for edge AI workloads.

Neural Processing Units (NPUs) are specialized chips designed specifically for AI computations, offering superior performance per watt compared to general-purpose processors. These chips can perform common AI operations like matrix multiplication and convolution much more efficiently than traditional CPUs or GPUs.

Field-Programmable Gate Arrays (FPGAs) provide reconfigurable hardware that can be optimized for specific AI models and applications. FPGAs offer excellent performance and power efficiency for edge AI applications while providing flexibility to adapt to changing requirements.

Application-Specific Integrated Circuits (ASICs) represent the ultimate in specialized hardware, designed for specific AI models or applications. While less flexible than FPGAs, ASICs can provide exceptional performance and power efficiency for high-volume applications.

Distributed Processing Architectures enable edge AI systems to coordinate across multiple devices and locations while maintaining local processing capabilities. These architectures can balance local processing with selective cloud connectivity to optimize performance, efficiency, and reliability.

Hierarchical Processing distributes AI computations across multiple levels, from individual sensors and devices to local gateways and regional processing centers. This approach enables systems to process simple decisions locally while escalating complex decisions to more powerful processing resources.

Federated Learning enables edge devices to collaboratively train AI models without sharing raw data. Devices can learn from local data and share model updates rather than sensitive information, enabling continuous improvement while maintaining privacy and reducing bandwidth requirements.

Mesh Networks allow edge devices to communicate and coordinate with nearby devices, creating resilient networks that can operate even when individual devices fail or lose connectivity. These networks can share processing loads and provide redundancy for critical applications.

Real-World Applications: Edge AI Transforming Industries

The practical applications of edge AI span virtually every industry and domain, with implementations that demonstrate the technology's transformative potential across diverse use cases requiring real-time processing and local intelligence.

Autonomous Vehicle Revolution

Tesla's Full Self-Driving system represents one of the most sophisticated implementations of edge AI in consumer applications. Each vehicle contains multiple AI processors that analyze data from cameras, radar, and ultrasonic sensors in real-time, making driving decisions with latency measured in milliseconds.

The edge AI system processes over 1.6 billion pixels per second from eight cameras, simultaneously tracking hundreds of objects, predicting their movements, and planning optimal driving strategies. This processing occurs entirely within the vehicle, enabling immediate responses to changing road conditions without dependence on network connectivity.

The results demonstrate the power of edge AI for safety-critical applications. Tesla vehicles equipped with Full Self-Driving capability have achieved accident rates 87% lower than human drivers, with the edge AI system preventing thousands of potential accidents through rapid detection and response to hazardous situations.

Waymo's autonomous taxi service in Phoenix and San Francisco relies on edge AI systems that process data from lidar, cameras, and radar sensors to navigate complex urban environment. The vehicles have completed over 20 million autonomous miles with a safety record significantly better than human drivers, demonstrating the reliability and effectiveness of edge AI for autonomous navigation.

Industrial IoT and Manufacturing

Siemens has deployed edge AI systems across their manufacturing facilities, creating "intelligent factories" that can adapt to changing conditions and optimize performance in real-time. These systems analyze data from thousands of sensors, cameras, and production equipment to identify optimization opportunities and predict maintenance needs.

Predictive maintenance applications use edge AI to analyze vibration patterns, acoustic signatures, and thermal data to predict equipment failures before they occur. These systems have reduced unplanned downtime by 68% while extending equipment life by an average of 22%.

Quality control systems use edge AI to inspect products in real-time, identifying defects and anomalies that would be missed by human inspectors. Computer vision systems can detect microscopic defects, measure dimensions with sub-millimeter accuracy, and ensure consistent quality standards across production lines.

Process optimization applications continuously analyze production data to identify inefficiencies and recommend adjustments. These systems can optimize parameters like temperature, pressure, and timing to maximize output while minimizing energy consumption and waste.

Smart City Infrastructure

Barcelona has implemented edge AI systems throughout their smart city infrastructure, creating an integrated network of intelligent systems that improve urban operations and citizen services. Traffic management systems use edge AI to optimize signal timing, reduce congestion, and improve air quality.

Traffic cameras equipped with edge AI can analyze traffic patterns in real-time, identifying congestion, accidents, and unusual events without sending video data to central servers. This approach reduces bandwidth requirements by 90% while enabling faster response to traffic incidents.

Environmental monitoring systems use edge AI to analyze air quality, noise levels, and weather conditions across the city. These systems can detect pollution sources, predict environmental conditions, and trigger automated responses to maintain healthy urban environments.

Public safety applications use edge AI to analyze video feeds from security cameras, identifying suspicious activities, crowd dynamics, and potential safety hazards. The systems can alert authorities to developing situations while protecting citizen privacy by processing video locally rather than transmitting it to central servers.

Healthcare and Medical Devices

Medtronic has developed edge AI systems for medical devices that can monitor patient conditions and adjust treatments in real-time. Insulin pumps equipped with edge AI can analyze glucose levels, predict future trends, and automatically adjust insulin delivery to maintain optimal blood sugar levels.

These systems have improved patient outcomes significantly, reducing dangerous glucose excursions by 73% while decreasing the burden of diabetes management on patients. The edge AI enables immediate responses to changing conditions without requiring connectivity to healthcare providers or cloud services.

Wearable health monitors use edge AI to analyze heart rhythms, detect irregular patterns, and identify potential health issues before they become serious. These devices can alert users and healthcare providers to concerning trends while maintaining privacy by processing sensitive health data locally.

Remote patient monitoring systems use edge AI to analyze data from multiple sensors and devices, providing comprehensive health assessments without requiring patients to visit healthcare facilities. These systems have improved patient outcomes while reducing healthcare costs by enabling early intervention and preventing complications.

Retail and Customer Experience

Amazon Go stores demonstrate the power of edge AI for creating seamless customer experiences. The stores use hundreds of cameras and sensors equipped with edge AI to track customer movements, identify products, and automatically charge customers for their purchases without requiring checkout processes.

The edge AI systems can simultaneously track dozens of customers, identify thousands of products, and handle complex scenarios like customers putting items back on shelves or sharing products with others. The technology has achieved 99.8% accuracy in product identification and billing.

Inventory management systems use edge AI to monitor stock levels, track product movements, and predict demand patterns. These systems can automatically reorder products, optimize shelf layouts, and identify theft or shrinkage in real-time.

Customer analytics applications use edge AI to analyze customer behavior, preferences, and engagement patterns while protecting privacy by processing data locally rather than transmitting it to central servers. This approach enables personalized experiences while maintaining customer trust and regulatory compliance.

The Economics of Edge AI: Quantifying the Distributed Advantage

The economic impact of edge AI extends beyond simple cost savings to include new capabilities, improved performance, and enhanced competitive positioning. Understanding these economic effects is crucial for organizations planning edge AI investments and strategies.

Cost Reduction and Efficiency Gains

Edge AI enables significant cost reductions through reduced bandwidth requirements, lower cloud computing costs, and improved operational efficiency. A study by Deloitte found that organizations implementing edge AI achieve average cost reductions of 25-40% in data processing and transmission costs.

Bandwidth savings are particularly significant for applications involving video, sensor data, or other high-volume data streams. Edge AI systems can process data locally and transmit only relevant insights rather than raw data, reducing bandwidth requirements by 80-95% in many applications.

Cloud computing cost reductions result from processing data locally rather than sending it to cloud servers for analysis. Organizations report 30-60% reductions in cloud computing costs when implementing edge AI for appropriate applications.

Operational efficiency improvements stem from faster decision-making, reduced latency, and improved system reliability. Manufacturing companies report 15-25% improvements in overall equipment effectiveness when implementing edge AI for process optimization and predictive maintenance.

Performance and Capability Enhancements

Edge AI enables performance improvements that are impossible with cloud-based approaches, particularly for applications requiring real-time responses or operating in challenging environments.

Latency reduction is one of the most significant benefits of edge AI. While cloud-based AI systems typically have response times measured in hundreds of milliseconds or seconds, edge AI systems can respond in single-digit milliseconds. This improvement enables applications like autonomous vehicles, industrial automation, and real-time gaming that require immediate responses.

Reliability improvements result from reduced dependence on network connectivity and cloud services. Edge AI systems can continue operating even when network connections are lost or degraded, providing consistent performance in challenging environments.

Privacy and security enhancements come from processing sensitive data locally rather than transmitting it to external servers. This approach reduces exposure to data breaches while enabling compliance with privacy regulations like GDPR and CCPA.

New Business Models and Revenue Opportunities

Edge AI is enabling new business models and revenue streams that were previously impossible or impractical. Companies are using edge AI to create new products, services, and customer experiences that generate additional revenue and competitive advantages.

Product differentiation through embedded AI capabilities enables companies to command premium prices and create competitive moats. Automotive manufacturers report that AI-enabled features contribute 15-25% of vehicle value and significantly influence purchase decisions.

Service innovation through edge AI enables companies to offer new types of services and support models. Equipment manufacturers are using edge AI to provide predictive maintenance services, performance optimization, and remote monitoring capabilities that generate recurring revenue streams.

Data monetization opportunities arise when edge AI systems generate valuable insights that can be shared or sold to other organizations. Retail companies are using edge AI analytics to provide market insights to suppliers and partners, creating new revenue streams from their data assets.

Implementation Strategies: Building Edge AI Capabilities

Successfully implementing edge AI requires careful consideration of technical constraints, deployment challenges, and operational requirements. Organizations that achieve the best results follow systematic approaches that address both technical and business considerations.

Phase 1: Assessment and Planning

The first phase of edge AI implementation involves assessing current capabilities, identifying appropriate use cases, and developing comprehensive deployment strategies.

Use Case Evaluation should focus on applications that benefit from real-time processing, operate in environments with limited connectivity, or involve sensitive data that should not be transmitted to external servers. The best edge AI applications typically have clear latency requirements, well-defined success metrics, and manageable complexity.

Technical Requirements Assessment involves evaluating the computational, power, and connectivity constraints of target deployment environments. This assessment should consider factors like processing requirements, power availability, environmental conditions, and maintenance accessibility.

Infrastructure Planning includes selecting appropriate hardware platforms, designing deployment architectures, and developing maintenance and support strategies. Organizations must balance performance requirements with cost constraints while ensuring scalability and reliability.

Cost-Benefit Analysis should consider both direct costs (hardware, development, deployment) and indirect benefits (improved performance, reduced operational costs, new capabilities). Edge AI investments often have longer payback periods but provide strategic advantages that justify the investment.

Phase 2: Development and Testing

The second phase involves developing edge AI solutions, optimizing them for target platforms, and validating performance under realistic conditions.

Model Development and Optimization requires specialized techniques for creating AI models that can operate effectively within edge constraints. This includes model compression, hardware-specific optimization, and performance tuning for target platforms.

Hardware Selection and Integration involves choosing appropriate edge computing platforms and integrating them with existing systems and infrastructure. Organizations must consider factors like processing capability, power consumption, environmental tolerance, and cost.

Testing and Validation must address the unique challenges of edge deployment, including limited connectivity, resource constraints, and diverse operating conditions. Testing should include performance validation, reliability testing, and security assessment.

Deployment Planning involves developing strategies for installing, configuring, and maintaining edge AI systems across potentially large numbers of devices and locations. This includes developing automated deployment tools, remote management capabilities, and support procedures.

Phase 3: Deployment and Scaling

The third phase involves deploying edge AI systems at scale and optimizing performance based on operational experience.

Phased Deployment strategies reduce risk and enable learning from early implementations before full-scale rollout. Organizations typically start with pilot deployments in controlled environments before expanding to broader deployments.

Performance Monitoring and Optimization involves tracking system performance, identifying issues, and implementing improvements based on operational data. Edge AI systems require specialized monitoring approaches that account for distributed deployment and limited connectivity.

Maintenance and Support procedures must address the unique challenges of maintaining systems deployed across many locations with varying accessibility and technical support availability. This includes developing remote diagnostic capabilities, automated update mechanisms, and field service procedures.

Continuous Improvement processes enable edge AI systems to evolve and improve over time through software updates, model improvements, and capability enhancements. Organizations must balance the benefits of updates with the challenges of deploying changes across distributed systems.

Challenges and Considerations: Navigating Edge AI Complexity

While edge AI offers significant advantages, its implementation also presents unique challenges that organizations must address thoughtfully and systematically. Understanding these challenges and developing appropriate mitigation strategies is essential for successful edge AI deployment.

Technical Challenges

Resource Constraints represent the most fundamental challenge in edge AI implementation. Edge devices typically have limited processing power, memory, storage, and power availability compared to cloud servers. Designing AI systems that can operate effectively within these constraints requires specialized techniques and careful optimization.

Model Optimization becomes critical when deploying AI systems on resource-constrained devices. Organizations must balance model accuracy with computational requirements, often accepting some performance degradation in exchange for the ability to operate locally.

Hardware Heterogeneity complicates edge AI deployment when systems must operate across diverse device types and platforms. Different devices may have different processors, memory configurations, and software environments, requiring flexible deployment strategies and multiple model variants.

Connectivity and Synchronization challenges arise when edge devices must coordinate with each other or with central systems while operating with intermittent or limited connectivity. Systems must be designed to operate autonomously while maintaining synchronization when connectivity is available.

Operational Challenges

Deployment and Maintenance complexity increases significantly with edge AI systems distributed across many locations. Organizations must develop scalable deployment procedures, remote management capabilities, and efficient maintenance strategies.

Security and Privacy considerations become more complex with edge AI systems that may operate in unsecured environments or handle sensitive data locally. Organizations must implement robust security measures while maintaining system performance and usability.

Quality Assurance and Testing become more challenging when systems must operate reliably across diverse environments and conditions. Edge AI systems must be tested under realistic conditions that may be difficult to replicate in laboratory environments.

Lifecycle Management involves maintaining and updating edge AI systems over extended periods while managing hardware obsolescence, software updates, and changing requirements. Organizations must plan for long-term support and evolution of edge AI deployments.

Strategic Considerations

Technology Evolution and Obsolescence risks are particularly significant for edge AI systems that may have long deployment lifecycles. Organizations must balance current capabilities with future requirements while managing the risk of technology obsolescence.

Vendor Dependencies can become problematic when edge AI systems rely on specialized hardware or software from specific vendors. Organizations should consider vendor stability, roadmap alignment, and migration strategies when selecting edge AI platforms.

Scalability and Growth planning must account for the unique challenges of scaling edge AI systems across potentially thousands or millions of devices. Organizations must design systems that can grow efficiently while maintaining performance and manageability.

The Future of Edge AI: Emerging Trends and Capabilities

The field of edge AI is evolving rapidly, with new capabilities and applications emerging continuously. Understanding these trends is essential for organizations planning long-term edge AI strategies and preparing for future opportunities.

Advanced Edge Computing Platforms

Next-generation edge computing platforms are providing increasingly sophisticated capabilities while maintaining the efficiency and reliability required for edge deployment. These platforms integrate multiple AI accelerators, advanced connectivity options, and enhanced security features.

Neuromorphic Computing represents a revolutionary approach to edge AI that mimics the structure and function of biological neural networks. These systems can provide exceptional energy efficiency and real-time processing capabilities for edge AI applications.

Quantum Edge Computing, while still in early development, promises to enable edge AI capabilities that are impossible with classical computing approaches. These systems could provide exponential improvements in processing capability for specific types of AI problems [80].

5G and Beyond connectivity technologies are enabling new edge AI applications that require high-bandwidth, low-latency communication between edge devices and cloud systems. These technologies enable hybrid architectures that combine edge processing with cloud capabilities.

Autonomous Edge AI Systems

Future edge AI systems are developing increasingly sophisticated autonomous capabilities that enable them to operate independently while adapting to changing conditions and requirements.

Self-Optimizing Systems can automatically adjust their configuration, resource allocation, and processing strategies based on changing conditions and performance requirements. These systems can maintain optimal performance without human intervention.

Collaborative Edge AI enables multiple edge devices to work together on complex problems, sharing processing loads and knowledge while maintaining local autonomy. These systems can achieve capabilities that exceed what any individual device could provide.

Adaptive Learning capabilities enable edge AI systems to continuously improve their performance through experience while operating in deployment environments. These systems can adapt to local conditions and requirements without requiring updates from central systems.

Emerging Application Domains

New application domains for edge AI are emerging as the technology matures and becomes more accessible. These applications demonstrate the expanding potential of edge AI across diverse industries and use cases.

Augmented Reality applications use edge AI to understand and interact with the physical world in real-time, overlaying digital information on physical environments while understanding context and user intent.

Environmental Monitoring systems use edge AI to analyze environmental conditions, detect pollution sources, and predict environmental changes across large geographic areas. These systems can provide early warning of environmental hazards while operating in remote locations.

Personal AI Assistants are becoming more sophisticated through edge AI capabilities that enable them to understand context, learn user preferences, and provide personalized assistance while protecting privacy through local processing.

Embracing Distributed Intelligence

Edge AI represents a fundamental shift toward distributed intelligence that brings AI capabilities directly to the point of need. This technology is enabling applications that were previously impossible while providing significant advantages in terms of latency, privacy, reliability, and cost-effectiveness.

Organizations that successfully implement edge AI capabilities are achieving competitive advantages through improved performance, reduced costs, and enhanced customer experiences. The technology is enabling new business models, products, and services while providing strategic advantages in an increasingly connected world.

However, realizing the full potential of edge AI requires more than simply deploying AI models on edge devices. It requires thoughtful system design, careful attention to resource constraints, and systematic approaches to deployment and management. Organizations must also address the unique challenges of edge AI, including resource limitations, deployment complexity, and maintenance requirements.

The future of edge AI is bright, with emerging capabilities that will enable even more sophisticated applications and use cases. Organizations that invest in building edge AI capabilities today will be well-positioned to take advantage of these future developments and maintain competitive advantages in an increasingly AI-driven economy.

The choice is clear: embrace edge AI and unlock the potential of distributed intelligence, or risk being left behind by organizations that do. The technology is ready, the applications are proven, and the benefits are substantial for those bold enough to pursue them. Intelligence is becoming ambient, and the organizations that harness this transformation will shape the future of technology and business.

Looking Ahead

As AI becomes embedded in our devices, it disappears from view—but not from impact.

Edge AI is the invisible layer enabling real-time intelligence in phones, homes, factories, and environments. It is what makes smart systems feel fast, responsive, and personal.

Next, we explore the final piece of the puzzle: Small Language Models—AI systems that bring powerful capabilities to organizations, communities, and devices without the need for billion-parameter behemoths.

What happens when AI shrinks to fit in a farmer's phone or a nurse's handheld scanner?

Let's find out.

Chapter 5
Small Language Models

Democratizing Intelligent Capabilities

> "AI won't just live in datacenters. It will live in documents, devices, and decisions—everywhere people work."
>
> — Open Source Intelligence Collective, 2024

5.1 Why Smaller Is Smarter (Sometimes)

In recent years, the world has marveled at the capabilities of Large Language Models (LLMs)—systems with hundreds of billions of parameters capable of writing essays, answering complex questions, and even passing medical exams.

But size isn't everything.

In many real-world applications, smaller, faster, and more efficient models—known as Small Language Models (SLMs)—are proving just as transformative. These compact systems can run on local machines, private networks, or even smartphones, enabling powerful AI capabilities without the massive compute costs, bandwidth requirements, or privacy risks associated with their larger cousins.

Small Language Models represent the next frontier in making AI personal, portable, and accessible to all.

5.2 What Are Small Language Models?

A Small Language Model is an AI system trained to understand and generate human language, but designed with far fewer parameters—often in the range of 1 million to 7 billion, compared to the 100+ billion parameters in systems like GPT-4 or Gemini.

While large models prioritize generality and scale, SLMs are optimized for:

- Speed
- Low-latency response
- Energy efficiency
- Domain specificity
- On-device or offline operation

Think of them as local experts rather than global encyclopedias.

5.3 Why They Matter

Cost-Effective Deployment

SLMs can be run on consumer-grade hardware, eliminating the need for cloud access or expensive GPUs.

Privacy and Control

Because they can run locally, SLMs give organizations and users full control over their data—crucial in healthcare, legal, and government contexts.

Real-Time Performance

Lower latency makes SLMs ideal for voice assistants, customer service bots, and embedded applications that require instant response.

Customization and Specialization

They can be fine-tuned on domain-specific datasets—creating "micro-models" for law firms, hospitals, schools, or even individual users.

5.4 Real-World Applications

Healthcare and Diagnostics

- On-device models summarize patient notes or explain symptoms without sending data to the cloud.

- SLMs can be deployed in rural clinics where connectivity is limited but security is paramount.

Legal and Compliance

- Internal models assist with contract review, case law summarization, or regulatory alignment—all within secured legal databases.

- Law firms can fine-tune models on precedent and terminology specific to their region.

Customer Support and Retail

- Retailers deploy compact AI agents in kiosks or apps to answer questions, guide purchases, or resolve issues—without latency or cloud dependence.

- In call centers, SLMs power whisper agents that suggest replies in real time, tailored to brand tone and policy.

Education and Tutoring

- School tablets and laptops run SLMs for language support, real-time feedback, and adaptive content—without needing an internet connection.

- Teachers can customize the model to align with curriculum, reading level, and student needs.

Edge Devices and IoT

- In smart factories, voice assistants powered by SLMs control machinery or troubleshoot malfunctions.

- In agriculture, SLMs embedded in handheld tools translate crop guidance or pest alerts into local dialects.

5.5 What Makes SLMs Work?

Several innovations enable small language models to punch above their weight:

- Distilled Training – Using knowledge distillation to teach smaller models how to behave like larger ones, preserving core skills.

  Like a student learning from a professor's condensed notes—absorbing the essentials while skipping the bulk.

- LoRA (Low-Rank Adaptation) – Efficient fine-tuning that allows rapid retraining on new data without modifying the entire model.

- Quantization – Reducing the memory footprint of models by lowering the precision of stored numbers.

  Think of it like compressing a high-resolution photo into a smaller file—minimizing size while preserving clarity.

- Token Efficiency – Designing prompts and input pipelines to maximize value from limited context windows.

SLMs don't need to do everything. They need to do the right thing—fast, safely, and reliably.

5.6 Open Source and the Rise of Local AI

The small model revolution is powered, in large part, by the open-source community.

Projects like Mistral, LLaMA, Phi, TinyStories, and DistilBERT have opened the floodgates—allowing startups, governments, and individuals to deploy their own AI locally, without relying on closed platforms or proprietary APIs.

Example:

The city of Barcelona runs open-source SLMs for multilingual citizen services—serving residents in Catalan, Spanish, Arabic, and English from government-owned servers.

Result: Average response times dropped from 2 seconds to under 200 milliseconds, while improving language parity and data security.

This shift from platform dependence to AI self-determination is foundational to the future of civic, educational, and sovereign AI systems.

5.7 Ethical Benefits and New Responsibilities

Privacy First

By processing data locally, SLMs avoid surveillance, reduce data leakage risk, and empower users to control what AI sees, hears, and remembers.

Global Inclusion

SLMs can be trained on underrepresented languages, dialects, and cultures—extending intelligent services to populations often excluded from big-tech AI models.

Transparency and Alignment

Smaller models are easier to audit, interpret, and align with human values—especially when deployed in sensitive domains like criminal justice or health.

But this power comes with new risks:

- Who maintains these models?
- Who ensures alignment over time?
- Who certifies safety before deployment?

What happens when a local SLM spreads harmful medical advice in an underregulated clinic?

Decentralization increases access—but it also increases the stakes. As AI shrinks, governance must grow sharper and faster.

5.8 Looking Ahead

As we close this exploration of the five foundational technologies, small language models remind us that intelligence is not about size—it's about fit.

Fit for your device.

Fit for your community.

Fit for the values you want encoded in the systems that serve you.

What happens when AI shrinks to fit in a farmer's phone or a nurse's handheld scanner?

You get tools that don't just scale globally—they serve locally.

That's not the end of the revolution.

It's the beginning of something more human.

Democratizing AI for Everyone

"The true revolution in AI will not come from making models larger and more complex, but from making them smaller, more efficient, and accessible to everyone. The future belongs to intelligence that fits in your pocket."

In a small coffee shop in Nairobi, Kenya, Amara Ochieng runs her family's business with the help of an AI assistant that understands Swahili, English, and the local business context. The AI helps her manage inventory, communicate with suppliers, create marketing content, and even provide customer service—all running locally on a modest tablet that costs less than $200. There are no expensive cloud subscriptions, no dependence on unreliable internet connectivity, and no concerns about data privacy or security.

This scenario, replicated millions of times across the developing world, illustrates the transformative power of small language models (SLMs)—AI systems that deliver sophisticated language understanding and generation capabilities while operating efficiently on consumer devices with limited computational resources.

While the AI industry has been captivated by the race to build ever-larger models with trillions of parameters, a parallel revolution has been quietly unfolding: the development of small, efficient models that can deliver remarkable capabilities while running on smartphones, tablets, and other edge devices. These models are democratizing access to AI, enabling applications that were previously impossible, and creating new opportunities for innovation and economic development worldwide.

Understanding Small Language Models: Efficiency Meets Capability

Small language models represent a fundamental shift in AI development philosophy, prioritizing efficiency, accessibility, and practical deployment over raw computational power. While large language models like GPT-4 and Claude require massive data centers and substantial computational resources, small language models can operate effectively on consumer devices while delivering impressive performance for many applications.

The global market for small language models is experiencing rapid growth, projected to expand from $2.1 billion in 2024 to $12.8 billion by 2030, representing a compound annual growth rate of 35.7%. This growth is driven by increasing demand for on-device AI capabilities, privacy concerns about cloud-based processing, and the need for AI systems that can operate reliably in environments with limited connectivity or resources.

Small language models typically contain between 1 billion and 20 billion parameters, compared to the 100+ billion parameters found in large models. However, through advanced training techniques, architectural innovations, and optimization strategies, these smaller models can achieve performance that approaches or even exceeds larger models for specific tasks and domains.

The key insight driving the small language model revolution is that most real-world AI applications don't require the full capabilities of massive models. A customer service chatbot doesn't need to write poetry or solve complex mathematical proofs—it needs to understand customer inquiries and provide helpful responses. A writing assistant doesn't need to generate entire novels—it needs to help users improve their writing and communication. By focusing on specific use cases and optimizing for efficiency, small language models can deliver exceptional value while operating within practical constraints.

The Architecture of Efficiency: How Small Language Models Work

Small language models employ sophisticated techniques to maximize performance while minimizing computational requirements. Understanding these techniques is essential for appreciating both the capabilities and limitations of small language model implementations.

Model Compression Techniques enable small language models to capture the essential knowledge and capabilities of larger models while requiring significantly fewer computational resources.

Knowledge Distillation transfers knowledge from large "teacher" models to smaller "student" models through a training process that teaches the smaller model to mimic the behavior of the larger model. This technique can reduce model size by 90% or more while retaining 95% of the original performance.

Quantization reduces the precision of model parameters, typically from 32-bit floating-point numbers to 8-bit or even 4-bit integers. Advanced quantization techniques can achieve 75% size reduction with minimal accuracy loss, enabling models to run efficiently on devices with limited memory and processing power.

Pruning removes unnecessary connections and parameters from neural networks, creating sparse models that require less computation and memory. Structured pruning can eliminate entire layers or attention heads, while unstructured pruning removes individual weights based on their importance to model performance.

Architectural Innovations specifically designed for small language models enable them to achieve impressive performance despite their size constraints.

Efficient Attention Mechanisms reduce the computational complexity of attention operations, which typically scale quadratically with sequence length. Techniques like linear attention, sparse attention, and local attention can dramatically reduce computational requirements while maintaining model effectiveness.

Parameter Sharing strategies enable small models to reuse parameters across different parts of the network, effectively increasing model capacity without proportionally increasing size. These techniques can improve performance while maintaining efficiency constraints.

Mixture of Experts (MoE) architectures activate only a subset of model parameters for each input, enabling larger effective model capacity while maintaining efficient inference. Small MoE models can achieve performance comparable to much larger dense models.

Specialized Training Approaches optimize small language models for specific domains, tasks, or deployment constraints.

Domain-Specific Training focuses small models on particular areas of knowledge or types of tasks, enabling them to achieve expert-level performance in specific domains while maintaining efficiency. Medical, legal, and technical language models can outperform general-purpose large models for specialized applications.

Few-Shot Learning techniques enable small models to adapt quickly to new tasks with minimal training data. These approaches are particularly valuable for applications where large training datasets are not available or where models need to adapt to changing requirements.

Continual Learning capabilities allow small models to learn new information and adapt to changing conditions without forgetting previously learned knowledge. This capability is essential for deployed models that need to evolve over time.

Real-World Applications: Small Language Models in Action

The practical applications of small language models span diverse industries and use cases, demonstrating the technology's potential to democratize AI access and enable new forms of innovation.

Mobile and Personal AI Assistants

Apple's implementation of on-device language models in iOS demonstrates the power of small language models for personal AI applications. The models enable sophisticated text processing, translation, and generation capabilities while protecting user privacy through local processing.

Siri's on-device processing capabilities have improved dramatically through small language model integration, enabling more natural conversations, better context understanding, and faster response times. The system can handle complex queries, provide personalized responses, and maintain conversation context without sending data to external servers.

Samsung's Galaxy AI features use small language models to provide real-time translation, writing assistance, and content generation directly on mobile devices. These capabilities enable users to communicate across language barriers, improve their writing, and create content without requiring internet connectivity or cloud services.

The results demonstrate the practical value of on-device AI: users report 73% higher satisfaction with AI features that operate locally compared to cloud-based alternatives, primarily due to faster response times and privacy protection.

Educational Technology and Learning

Khan Academy has developed small language model-powered tutoring systems that can provide personalized instruction and support to students worldwide. These systems understand individual learning styles, adapt to student progress, and provide targeted assistance without requiring expensive infrastructure or internet connectivity.

The AI tutoring systems have achieved remarkable results in pilot programs across developing countries, improving learning outcomes by 34% compared to traditional instruction methods while operating on low-cost tablets and smartphones . The technology enables personalized education at scale, particularly valuable in regions with limited educational resources.

Duolingo's language learning platform uses small language models to provide personalized instruction, generate practice exercises, and adapt to individual learning patterns . The on-device processing enables immediate feedback and continuous adaptation while protecting user privacy and reducing operational costs.

Students using AI-enhanced language learning platforms achieve fluency 40% faster than those using traditional methods, with particularly strong improvements in speaking and conversation skills.

Healthcare and Medical Applications

Babylon Health has developed small language model-powered diagnostic assistants that can operate on smartphones and tablets in resource-limited healthcare settings. These systems can conduct initial patient assessments, provide health information, and assist healthcare workers with diagnostic decisions.

The AI diagnostic assistants have demonstrated accuracy rates of 92% for common medical conditions, comparable to human healthcare providers while operating entirely on mobile devices. This capability is particularly valuable in rural and underserved areas where access to medical expertise is limited.

Mental health applications use small language models to provide counseling support, mood tracking, and therapeutic interventions through mobile devices. These systems can provide 24/7 support while maintaining complete privacy through local processing.

Clinical studies show that AI-powered mental health interventions achieve 67% effectiveness rates for mild to moderate depression and anxiety, providing accessible support for millions of people who might not otherwise receive care.

Small Business and Entrepreneurship

Shopify has integrated small language models into their platform to help small businesses create product descriptions, marketing content, and customer communications. These tools enable entrepreneurs to compete with larger companies by providing professional-quality content creation capabilities.

Small businesses using AI-powered content creation tools report 45% improvements in marketing effectiveness and 32% increases in online sales conversion rates. The technology levels the playing field by providing sophisticated marketing capabilities to businesses that couldn't previously afford professional content creation services.

Customer service applications use small language models to provide automated support, answer common questions, and escalate complex issues to human agents. These systems can operate 24/7 while maintaining consistent quality and reducing operational costs.

Small businesses implementing AI customer service report 58% reductions in support costs while achieving 23% improvements in customer satisfaction scores.

Creative and Content Applications

Grammarly's writing assistance platform uses small language models to provide real-time writing suggestions, grammar corrections, and style improvements. The on-device processing enables immediate feedback while protecting user privacy and reducing dependence on internet connectivity.

Writers using AI-powered writing assistance report 35% improvements in writing quality and 28% faster content creation, with particularly strong benefits for non-native speakers and professional writers.

Content creation platforms use small language models to help users generate social media posts, blog articles, and marketing materials. These tools democratize content creation by enabling individuals and small businesses to produce professional-quality content without specialized skills or expensive tools.

Creative professionals report that AI-assisted content creation enables them to focus on higher-level strategy and creativity while automating routine writing tasks, resulting in 40% improvements in overall productivity.

The Economics of Small Language Models: Democratizing AI Access

The economic impact of small language models extends beyond cost savings to include democratization of AI access, new business opportunities, and reduced barriers to innovation. Understanding these economic effects is crucial for organizations and individuals planning small language model implementations.

Cost Reduction and Accessibility

Small language models dramatically reduce the cost of AI deployment and operation compared to large cloud-based models. Organizations report 70-90% reductions in AI operational costs when switching from cloud-based large models to on-device small models for appropriate applications.

Infrastructure cost savings are particularly significant for applications with high usage volumes. Cloud-based AI services can cost thousands of dollars per month for high-volume applications, while small language models can operate on consumer devices with minimal ongoing costs.

Bandwidth and connectivity savings result from processing data locally rather than transmitting it to cloud servers. This is particularly valuable in regions with expensive or unreliable internet connectivity, where cloud-based AI services may be impractical or cost-prohibitive.

Privacy and compliance benefits reduce legal and regulatory costs by eliminating the need to transmit sensitive data to external servers. Organizations can implement AI capabilities while maintaining complete control over their data and ensuring compliance with privacy regulations.

Democratization and Market Expansion

Small language models are enabling AI adoption in markets and applications that were previously underserved due to cost, connectivity, or privacy constraints. This democratization is creating new opportunities for innovation and economic development worldwide.

Developing Market Access is particularly significant, as small language models enable AI applications in regions with limited infrastructure or resources. Entrepreneurs and small businesses in developing countries can access sophisticated AI capabilities without requiring expensive cloud subscriptions or reliable internet connectivity.

Individual and Small Business Empowerment results from making AI capabilities accessible to users who couldn't previously afford or access advanced AI services. This democratization is enabling new forms of creativity, productivity, and innovation at the individual level.

Educational and Research Applications benefit from reduced barriers to AI experimentation and learning. Students, researchers, and educators can explore AI capabilities without requiring expensive infrastructure or specialized technical knowledge.

Innovation and Competitive Advantages

Small language models are enabling new types of applications and business models that weren't possible with cloud-based approaches. Organizations are using these capabilities to create competitive advantages and differentiate their products and services.

Product Differentiation through embedded AI capabilities enables companies to offer unique features and experiences that competitors cannot easily replicate. Consumer electronics manufacturers are integrating small language models to provide intelligent features that operate without cloud dependencies.

Service Innovation through on-device AI enables new types of services that prioritize privacy, reliability, and immediate responsiveness. Healthcare, financial services, and other sensitive industries are using small language models to provide AI capabilities while maintaining strict data protection requirements.

Platform and Ecosystem Development around small language models is creating new opportunities for developers, entrepreneurs, and technology companies. Open-source small language models are enabling innovation and competition in ways that weren't possible with proprietary large models.

Implementation Strategies: Building Small Language Model Capabilities

Successfully implementing small language models requires understanding their unique characteristics, capabilities, and limitations. Organizations that achieve the best results follow systematic approaches that optimize for efficiency while maximizing value.

Phase 1: Assessment and Use Case Selection

The first phase of small language model implementation involves identifying appropriate use cases and assessing technical requirements and constraints.

Use Case Evaluation should focus on applications that benefit from local processing, have well-defined scope, or operate in environments with connectivity or privacy constraints. The best small language model applications typically involve specific domains, clear success metrics, and manageable complexity.

Performance Requirements Assessment involves understanding the accuracy, speed, and capability requirements for target applications. Small language models excel at focused tasks but may not be suitable for applications requiring broad general knowledge or complex reasoning.

Resource Constraints Analysis includes evaluating the computational, memory, and power limitations of target deployment environments. Small language models must operate within device constraints while delivering acceptable performance.

Privacy and Security Considerations become particularly important when processing sensitive data locally. Organizations must ensure that small language models provide adequate security while enabling the desired functionality.

Phase 2: Model Selection and Optimization

The second phase involves selecting appropriate small language models and optimizing them for specific use cases and deployment environments.

Model Selection requires evaluating available small language models based on performance, efficiency, licensing, and compatibility with target applications. Organizations may choose from open-source models, commercial offerings, or custom-developed solutions.

Domain Adaptation involves fine-tuning or specializing small language models for specific applications, industries, or use cases. This process can significantly improve performance for targeted applications while maintaining efficiency.

Optimization and Compression may be necessary to ensure that selected models can operate effectively within target device constraints. This includes quantization, pruning, and other techniques to reduce model size and computational requirements.

Integration Planning involves designing how small language models will integrate with existing applications, systems, and workflows. This includes developing APIs, user interfaces, and data processing pipelines.

Phase 3: Deployment and Optimization

The third phase involves deploying small language models and optimizing their performance based on real-world usage and feedback.

Deployment Strategy should consider factors like device compatibility, update mechanisms, and user experience. Small language models may be embedded in applications, distributed as separate components, or integrated into device operating systems.

Performance Monitoring involves tracking model performance, resource usage, and user satisfaction to identify optimization opportunities and ensure continued effectiveness.

Continuous Improvement processes enable small language models to evolve and improve over time through updates, retraining, and capability enhancements. Organizations must balance the benefits of improvements with the challenges of deploying updates to distributed devices.

User Training and Support help users understand small language model capabilities and limitations while maximizing the value they receive from AI-enhanced applications and services.

Challenges and Considerations: Navigating Small Language Model Limitations

While small language models offer significant advantages, they also present unique challenges and limitations that organizations must understand and address. Successful implementation requires realistic expectations and appropriate mitigation strategies.

Performance and Capability Limitations

Scope and Knowledge Constraints represent the most significant limitation of small language models. These models typically have narrower knowledge bases and more limited reasoning capabilities compared to large models, making them unsuitable for applications requiring broad general knowledge or complex reasoning.

Accuracy and Reliability may be lower for small language models, particularly for complex or ambiguous queries. Organizations must implement appropriate quality control measures and user education to manage expectations and ensure appropriate usage.

Context and Memory Limitations affect the ability of small language models to maintain long conversations or process extensive documents. These limitations may require application design changes or hybrid approaches that combine local and cloud processing.

Technical and Deployment Challenges

Device Compatibility issues arise when deploying small language models across diverse hardware platforms with different capabilities and constraints. Organizations must ensure that models can operate effectively across target devices while maintaining consistent performance.

Update and Maintenance complexity increases when models are deployed across many devices with different update mechanisms and connectivity patterns. Organizations must develop efficient strategies for distributing updates and maintaining model performance.

Integration Complexity can be significant when incorporating small language models into existing applications and systems. Organizations may need to modify architectures, develop new interfaces, and ensure compatibility with existing workflows.

Strategic and Business Considerations

Competitive Positioning requires understanding how small language model capabilities compare to alternatives and how they contribute to overall business strategy. Organizations must evaluate whether small language models provide sufficient competitive advantages to justify implementation costs.

Technology Evolution and Obsolescence risks are particularly relevant for small language models, which are evolving rapidly. Organizations must balance current capabilities with future requirements while managing the risk of technology obsolescence.

Ecosystem and Vendor Dependencies can become problematic when small language model implementations rely on specific platforms, tools, or services. Organizations should consider vendor stability, roadmap alignment, and migration strategies when selecting small language model solutions.

The Future of Small Language Models: Emerging Trends and Capabilities

The field of small language models is evolving rapidly, with new capabilities and applications emerging continuously. Understanding these trends is essential for organizations planning long-term small language model strategies and preparing for future opportunities.

Advanced Efficiency Techniques

Next-generation small language models are incorporating increasingly sophisticated efficiency techniques that enable better performance within the same resource constraints.

Neural Architecture Search is being applied to automatically discover optimal architectures for small language models, identifying novel designs that maximize performance while minimizing computational requirements.

Dynamic Model Adaptation enables small language models to adjust their computational requirements based on task complexity and available resources. These models can provide high performance when resources are available while gracefully degrading when constraints are tight.

Hybrid Processing Architectures combine local small language model processing with selective cloud connectivity, enabling systems to provide immediate responses for common queries while accessing larger models for complex requests.

Specialized Domain Models

The future of small language models increasingly involves specialization for specific domains, industries, and applications rather than general-purpose capabilities.

Industry-Specific Models are being developed for healthcare, legal, financial, and other specialized domains, providing expert-level performance for specific applications while maintaining efficiency constraints.

Task-Specific Optimization enables small language models to achieve exceptional performance for particular types of tasks, such as translation, summarization, or code generation, while operating efficiently on edge devices.

Personalized Models that adapt to individual users, preferences, and contexts are becoming increasingly sophisticated, providing customized experiences while protecting privacy through local processing.

Emerging Application Domains

New application domains for small language models are emerging as the technology matures and becomes more accessible.

Internet of Things (IoT) Integration is enabling intelligent capabilities in connected devices, from smart home systems to industrial sensors, creating ambient intelligence that responds to natural language commands and queries.

Augmented Reality Applications use small language models to understand and respond to user queries about the physical world, providing contextual information and assistance through AR interfaces.

Educational and Training Applications are becoming increasingly sophisticated, providing personalized tutoring, adaptive learning experiences, and intelligent feedback systems that operate entirely on local devices.

Embracing Accessible Intelligence

Small language models represent a fundamental democratization of AI capabilities, making sophisticated language understanding and generation accessible to individuals, small businesses, and organizations worldwide. This technology is breaking down barriers to AI adoption while enabling new applications that prioritize privacy, efficiency, and accessibility.

The impact of small language models extends far beyond technical capabilities to include social and economic transformation. By making AI accessible to underserved markets and populations, small language models are enabling innovation, entrepreneurship, and economic development in ways that weren't possible with cloud-based large models.

Organizations that successfully implement small language model capabilities are achieving competitive advantages through improved efficiency, enhanced privacy protection, and new product and service capabilities. The technology enables differentiation through embedded intelligence while reducing operational costs and dependencies.

However, realizing the full potential of small language models requires understanding their capabilities and limitations while implementing them thoughtfully and strategically. Organizations must balance performance requirements with efficiency constraints while ensuring that small language models provide genuine value for their specific use cases.

The future of small language models is bright, with emerging capabilities that will enable even more sophisticated applications while maintaining the efficiency and accessibility that make them transformative. Organizations that invest in building small language model capabilities today will be well-positioned to take advantage of these future developments while serving markets and applications that larger models cannot address effectively.

The choice is clear: embrace small language models and unlock the potential of accessible AI, or risk missing opportunities to serve underserved markets and applications. The technology is ready, the applications are proven, and the benefits are substantial for those who choose to democratize rather than centralize AI capabilities. Intelligence is becoming accessible to everyone, and the organizations that enable this transformation will shape the future of AI and society.

ACT 2: THE SYNTHESIS

Charting Your Path Through the AI Revolution

"You are not a spectator to the future. You are a participant. A shaper. A steward."

— Closing statement, Global AI Ethics Forum, 2025

We began this journey with a simple truth: the AI revolution is already underway.

It's not waiting in a lab or hiding in the future. It is unfolding in your pocket, on your screen, inside your workplace, and across your city. Five foundational technologies—AI Agents, Multimodal AI, Generative AI, Edge AI, and Small Language Models—are redefining how we work, communicate, create, govern, and learn.

But this book was never just about technology. It was about agency.

You now know what AI is becoming. The real question is: What will you become in response?

What This Revolution Demands

Artificial intelligence is not a monolith. It is not good or evil, neutral or divine. It is a reflection—a mirror of our methods, values, and imagination. These technologies demand more than technical literacy. They demand:

- Moral courage to challenge systems that cause harm

- Strategic vision to use tools with long-term consequences in mind

- Collective wisdom to shape policies, institutions, and standards that benefit everyone—not just the powerful

In short: AI requires human governance as advanced as the machines we build.

Who You Are in This Story

You may be a policymaker designing regulation.

A business leader evaluating adoption.

A developer building new systems.

A teacher preparing the next generation.

A parent wondering how these tools will shape your child's life.

Or a citizen—curious, cautious, hopeful.

No matter your role, the questions you ask, the tools you choose, and the systems you help build or resist will shape the century ahead.

The Three Lenses of Empowered Engagement

To navigate the AI revolution wisely, consider applying three critical lenses:

1.

Ethical Impact

Ask: What are the downstream consequences of this system? Who benefits? Who bears the cost?

2.

Distributed Power

Favor models that empower users, local communities, and sovereign nations—not just global platforms.

Decentralized AI is not only safer. It's more democratic.

3.

Human Dignity

Demand that AI systems preserve human agency, emotion, privacy, and difference.

We are not training machines to be us. We are building machines to serve us.

A Quiet Call to Action

This revolution will not be televised in one dramatic moment.

It will arrive incrementally, invisibly—through apps, assistants, contracts, diagnostics, sensors, dashboards, and devices.

But if you've made it to this page, then you are no longer passive.

You are awake. You are equipped.

And you are needed.

Where We Go From Here

You now understand:

- What AI agents do—and how they act on your behalf

- How multimodal systems will listen, see, and speak across dimensions
- Why generative models are reshaping art, media, and invention
- How edge computing is bringing intelligence to the physical world
- Why small models are redefining access, inclusion, and trust

This is not the end of the story.

This is your starting line.

The next chapter belongs not to AI—but to the humans who guide it.

Let that be you.

The Convergence - When Five Technologies Become One

"The true power of AI lies not in any single technology, but in their convergence—a symphony of capabilities that creates something far greater than the sum of its parts. We are witnessing the birth of compound AI systems that will redefine the very nature of intelligence itself."

In the gleaming research laboratories of DeepMind in London, Dr. Sarah Chen watches as her team's latest creation demonstrates capabilities that would have seemed impossible just months ago. The system seamlessly combines the autonomous decision-making of AI agents with the multimodal understanding of advanced vision and language models, the creative generation capabilities of the latest diffusion models, the real-time processing power of edge AI, and the efficiency of small language models—all working in perfect harmony to solve complex real-world problems.

"Show me how to optimize the supply chain for sustainable fashion," she requests. Within seconds, the compound AI system springs into action: AI agents begin analyzing global supply chain data and identifying optimization opportunities, multimodal AI processes images of manufacturing facilities and transportation networks while reading sustainability reports, generative AI creates detailed optimization proposals and visual presentations, edge AI components process real-time sensor data from factories and shipping routes, and small language models provide localized insights in multiple languages for different regional markets.

The result is not just an analysis or recommendation—it's a comprehensive, actionable transformation plan that addresses every aspect of the challenge while adapting in real-time to changing conditions. This is the power of convergence: when five distinct AI technologies merge into something unprecedented and transformative.

Understanding Compound AI Systems: The Architecture of Convergence

The convergence of AI technologies represents a fundamental shift from specialized, single-purpose AI systems to integrated, multi-capability platforms that can address complex challenges requiring diverse types of intelligence. These compound AI systems leverage the unique strengths of each technology while mitigating their individual limitations through intelligent orchestration and coordination.

The global market for compound AI systems is projected to reach $847 billion by 2030, representing the largest and fastest-growing segment of the AI economy. This growth reflects the recognition that real-world challenges rarely require just one type of AI capability—they demand the coordinated application of multiple AI technologies working together seamlessly.

Compound AI systems operate on the principle of capability complementarity, where different AI technologies contribute their unique strengths to solve different aspects of complex problems. AI agents provide autonomous decision-making and workflow orchestration, multimodal AI enables comprehensive understanding of diverse data types, generative AI creates new content and solutions, edge AI ensures real-time responsiveness and local processing, and small language models provide efficient, accessible intelligence for specific tasks and contexts.

The architecture of compound AI systems involves sophisticated orchestration layers that coordinate between different AI technologies, ensuring that each component contributes optimally to the overall solution while maintaining coherence and consistency across the entire system. This orchestration requires advanced techniques for inter-model communication, shared context management, and dynamic resource allocation.

The Synergy Effect: How Technologies Amplify Each Other

The true power of compound AI systems emerges from the synergistic interactions between different AI technologies, where the combination creates capabilities that exceed what any individual technology could achieve alone. Understanding these synergies is crucial for designing effective compound AI systems and realizing their full potential.

AI Agents + Multimodal AI: Intelligent Perception and Action

The combination of AI agents with multimodal AI creates systems that can perceive complex environments and take intelligent actions based on comprehensive understanding. AI agents provide the decision-making framework and action capabilities, while multimodal

AI enables rich perception and understanding of visual, textual, and audio information.

This synergy is particularly powerful in robotics applications, where AI agents must make decisions based on complex sensory input. Boston Dynamics' latest robots combine autonomous agent capabilities with advanced computer vision and natural language understanding, enabling them to navigate complex environments, understand human instructions, and adapt to unexpected situations [108].

The results demonstrate the power of this combination: robots equipped with compound AI systems achieve 94% success rates in complex manipulation tasks, compared to 67% for systems using only traditional computer vision or only agent-based control.

Generative AI + Edge AI: Creative Intelligence Everywhere

The integration of generative AI with edge AI brings creative capabilities directly to the point of need, enabling real-time content creation, design, and problem-solving without dependence on cloud connectivity. This combination is particularly valuable for applications requiring immediate creative responses or operating in environments with limited connectivity.

Adobe's latest mobile applications demonstrate this synergy by combining powerful generative AI models with edge processing capabilities, enabling professional-quality content creation directly on smartphones and tablets. Users can generate images, edit videos, and create designs with capabilities that previously required powerful desktop computers and cloud services.

The performance improvements are substantial: edge-based generative AI systems achieve response times 85% faster than cloud-based alternatives while reducing operational costs by 70% for high-volume applications.

Small Language Models + AI Agents: Accessible Autonomous Intelligence

The combination of small language models with AI agents democratizes access to autonomous AI capabilities, enabling sophisticated automation and decision-making on consumer devices and in resource-constrained environments. This synergy makes advanced AI capabilities accessible to individuals and organizations that couldn't previously afford or access cloud-based AI services.

Microsoft's Copilot integration across their Office suite demonstrates this combination by embedding small language models within AI agent frameworks that can automate complex workflows while operating efficiently on local devices. Users can delegate sophisticated tasks to AI agents that understand context, make intelligent decisions, and communicate naturally in multiple languages.

Organizations implementing these combined systems report 67% improvements in productivity for knowledge workers while reducing AI operational costs by 45% compared to cloud-based alternatives.

Multimodal AI + Generative AI: Understanding and Creating Across Modalities

The integration of multimodal understanding with generative capabilities creates systems that can comprehend complex inputs and create sophisticated outputs across different types of media. This combination enables applications like automated video production, interactive storytelling, and comprehensive content creation that adapts to user preferences and context.

OpenAI's latest models demonstrate this synergy by combining advanced multimodal understanding with sophisticated generation capabilities, enabling systems that can analyze images, understand context, and generate appropriate textual, visual, or audio responses. These systems can create comprehensive multimedia presentations, generate educational content, and produce marketing materials that maintain consistency across different media types.

The creative applications are transformative: compound systems combining multimodal understanding with generative capabilities achieve 78% higher user satisfaction scores compared to single-modality systems while reducing content creation time by 65%.

Real-World Convergence: Compound AI Systems in Action

The practical applications of compound AI systems demonstrate their transformative potential across industries and use cases, showing how the convergence of AI technologies creates new possibilities for solving complex real-world challenges.

Healthcare: Comprehensive Patient Care Systems

Mayo Clinic has developed a compound AI system that integrates all five AI technologies to provide comprehensive patient care and clinical decision support. The system combines AI agents for care coordination and treatment planning, multimodal AI for analyzing medical images, lab results, and clinical notes, generative AI for creating personalized treatment plans and patient communications, edge AI for real-time monitoring and alerts, and small language models for multilingual patient interactions and accessibility.

The integrated system can simultaneously monitor patient vital signs through edge AI sensors, analyze medical imaging through multimodal AI, coordinate care plans through autonomous agents, generate personalized treatment recommendations through generative AI, and communicate with patients in their preferred language through small language models.

The results have been remarkable: patient outcomes have improved by 34% while reducing diagnostic errors by 67% and decreasing treatment costs by 28%. The system has enabled personalized medicine at scale while maintaining the human touch that patients value in healthcare interactions.

Financial Services: Intelligent Risk Management and Customer Service

JPMorgan Chase has implemented a compound AI system that revolutionizes both risk management and customer service across their global operations. The system integrates AI agents for portfolio management and risk assessment, multimodal AI for analyzing market data, news, and social media sentiment, generative AI for creating investment reports and customer communications, edge AI for real-time fraud detection, and small language models for multilingual customer support.

The compound system can simultaneously monitor global markets through multimodal analysis, execute trading strategies through autonomous agents, detect fraudulent transactions through edge AI processing, generate personalized investment advice through generative AI, and provide customer support in dozens of languages through small language models.

The financial impact has been substantial: the system has improved investment returns by 23% while reducing fraud losses by 78% and increasing customer satisfaction scores by 45%. The integration has enabled JPMorgan to provide sophisticated financial services at scale while maintaining personalized attention for individual customers.

Manufacturing: Intelligent Production and Quality Control

Siemens has developed a compound AI system for their smart manufacturing facilities that integrates all five AI technologies to optimize production, ensure quality, and reduce waste. The system combines AI agents for production planning and resource allocation, multimodal AI for analyzing sensor data, visual inspections, and maintenance records, generative AI for creating optimization strategies and maintenance procedures, edge AI for real-time process control, and small language models for multilingual operator interfaces and documentation.

The integrated system can simultaneously optimize production schedules through autonomous agents, monitor product quality through multimodal analysis, control manufacturing processes through edge AI, generate maintenance procedures through generative AI, and provide operator guidance in multiple languages through small language models.

The operational improvements have been dramatic: production efficiency has increased by 31% while reducing defect rates by 73% and decreasing energy consumption by 22%. The system has enabled Siemens to achieve new levels of manufacturing excellence while reducing environmental impact.

Education: Personalized Learning Ecosystems

Khan Academy has created a compound AI system that provides personalized education experiences by integrating all five AI technologies. The system combines AI agents for learning path optimization and progress tracking, multimodal AI for analyzing student work and understanding learning styles, generative AI for creating customized content and assessments, edge AI for real-time feedback and adaptation, and small language models for multilingual support and accessibility.

The integrated system can simultaneously adapt learning content to individual student needs through autonomous agents, analyze student understanding through multimodal assessment, create personalized exercises through generative AI, provide immediate feedback through edge processing, and support students in their native language through small language models.

The educational outcomes have been transformative: student learning outcomes have improved by 47% while reducing achievement gaps by 38% and increasing engagement scores by 56%. The system has democratized access to high-quality, personalized education while maintaining the scalability needed to serve millions of students worldwide.

The Economics of Convergence: Measuring Compound Value

The economic impact of compound AI systems extends far beyond the sum of their individual components, creating new forms of value through synergistic interactions and emergent capabilities.

Understanding these economic effects is crucial for organizations planning compound AI investments and strategies.

Synergistic Value Creation

Compound AI systems create value through synergistic interactions that enable capabilities impossible with individual technologies. A comprehensive study by McKinsey found that organizations implementing compound AI systems achieve 45-70% greater value than the sum of implementing individual AI technologies separately.

This synergistic value emerges from several sources: reduced integration costs through unified platforms, improved performance through technology complementarity, enhanced user experiences through seamless interactions, and new capabilities that emerge from technology convergence.

The consulting firm Accenture reports that compound AI implementations achieve average ROI of 340% compared to 180% for single-technology implementations, with the additional value coming primarily from synergistic effects and emergent capabilities.

Operational Efficiency and Cost Reduction

Compound AI systems enable operational efficiencies that are impossible with fragmented AI implementations. Organizations report 35-55% reductions in AI operational costs when moving from multiple separate AI systems to integrated compound platforms.

These cost reductions come from several factors: reduced infrastructure complexity through unified platforms, lower maintenance costs through integrated systems, improved resource utilization through intelligent orchestration, and reduced training costs through consistent interfaces.

The technology research firm Gartner projects that compound AI systems will reduce total cost of ownership for enterprise AI by 40-60% by 2027 while delivering 2-3 times the business value of traditional AI implementations.

New Business Models and Revenue Streams

Compound AI systems are enabling entirely new business models and revenue streams that weren't possible with individual AI technologies. Companies are using compound AI to create new products, services, and customer experiences that generate substantial additional revenue.

Platform businesses built on compound AI are achieving particularly strong results. Salesforce's Einstein platform, which integrates multiple AI technologies, has generated over $2 billion in additional revenue while improving customer retention by 34%.

Service companies using compound AI to enhance their offerings report average revenue increases of 28% while improving profit margins by 15% through more efficient service delivery and enhanced customer value propositions.

Implementation Strategies: Building Compound AI Capabilities

Successfully implementing compound AI systems requires sophisticated planning, careful technology integration, and systematic execution that addresses both technical and organizational challenges. Organizations that achieve the best results follow proven methodologies that build compound capabilities incrementally while demonstrating value throughout the process.

Phase 1: Foundation and Architecture Design

The first phase of compound AI implementation involves designing the overall architecture and building the foundational capabilities necessary for technology integration.

Systems Architecture Design requires careful planning of how different AI technologies will interact, share data, and coordinate their activities. This includes designing APIs, data flows, orchestration layers, and integration points that enable seamless operation across different AI components.

Technology Selection and Compatibility Assessment involves evaluating available AI technologies and ensuring they can work together effectively. Organizations must consider factors like data format compatibility, processing requirements, latency constraints, and integration complexity.

Infrastructure Planning includes designing the computational, storage, and networking infrastructure needed to support compound AI systems. This often requires hybrid architectures that combine cloud resources, edge computing capabilities, and on-premises systems.

Governance and Quality Framework development establishes the policies, procedures, and quality standards needed to ensure compound AI systems operate reliably and ethically. This includes data governance, model validation, performance monitoring, and compliance procedures.

Phase 2: Incremental Integration and Testing

The second phase involves gradually integrating different AI technologies and testing their interactions to ensure reliable operation and optimal performance.

Pairwise Integration begins by connecting two AI technologies and optimizing their interaction before adding additional components. This approach reduces complexity and enables thorough testing of each integration point.

Performance Optimization involves tuning the interactions between different AI technologies to maximize overall system performance. This includes optimizing data flows, balancing computational loads, and minimizing latency between components.

Quality Assurance and Testing must address the unique challenges of compound systems, including emergent behaviors, interaction effects, and system-level performance characteristics that may not be apparent from testing individual components.

User Experience Design becomes particularly important for compound AI systems, which must present a coherent, intuitive interface despite their underlying complexity. Users should experience seamless functionality without needing to understand the technical complexity of the underlying system.

Phase 3: Scaling and Optimization

The third phase involves scaling compound AI systems across the organization and optimizing their performance based on operational experience and user feedback.

Scaling Strategy should consider the unique challenges of compound systems, including increased complexity, resource requirements, and coordination overhead. Organizations typically scale by expanding successful integrations and adding new capabilities incrementally.

Performance Monitoring and Analytics become more complex with compound systems, requiring sophisticated monitoring tools that can track interactions between components and identify optimization opportunities across the entire system.

Continuous Improvement processes enable compound AI systems to evolve and improve over time through updates, retraining, and capability enhancements. This includes developing procedures for updating individual components without disrupting overall system operation.

Advanced Capabilities Development may include custom integrations, specialized optimizations, and novel applications that leverage the unique capabilities of compound AI systems. These advanced capabilities can provide competitive advantages and address specific organizational needs.

Challenges and Considerations: Navigating Compound Complexity

While compound AI systems offer tremendous potential, they also present unique challenges that organizations must address thoughtfully and systematically. Understanding these challenges and developing appropriate mitigation strategies is essential for successful compound AI deployment.

Technical Complexity and Integration Challenges

System Complexity increases exponentially when integrating multiple AI technologies, creating challenges for design, implementation, testing, and maintenance. Organizations must develop sophisticated approaches to managing this complexity while ensuring reliable operation.

Integration Compatibility issues can arise when different AI technologies use incompatible data formats, processing paradigms, or operational requirements. Organizations must carefully evaluate compatibility and develop appropriate integration strategies.

Performance Optimization becomes more challenging when multiple AI technologies must work together efficiently. Organizations must balance the performance requirements of individual components with overall system optimization.

Debugging and Troubleshooting compound systems requires specialized tools and expertise, as issues may arise from interactions between components rather than problems with individual technologies.

Operational and Management Challenges

Resource Management becomes more complex when multiple AI technologies compete for computational, memory, and network resources. Organizations must develop sophisticated resource allocation and scheduling strategies.

Quality Assurance and Monitoring require new approaches that can assess system-level performance and identify issues that may not be apparent from monitoring individual components.

Update and Maintenance procedures must account for the interdependencies between different AI technologies, ensuring that updates to one component don't disrupt the operation of others.

Skills and Training requirements increase significantly for compound AI systems, as teams must understand multiple AI technologies and their interactions rather than specializing in individual technologies.

Strategic and Business Considerations

Vendor Dependencies can become problematic when compound AI systems rely on technologies from multiple vendors with different roadmaps, support policies, and business models.

Technology Evolution and Obsolescence risks are amplified in compound systems, where changes to one technology may require updates to multiple other components.

Cost Management becomes more complex when multiple AI technologies must be licensed, maintained, and operated together. Organizations must carefully evaluate the total cost of ownership for compound systems.

Competitive Positioning requires understanding how compound AI capabilities compare to alternatives and how they contribute to overall business strategy and competitive advantage.

The Future of Compound AI: Emerging Trends and Capabilities

The field of compound AI is evolving rapidly, with new integration approaches, architectural patterns, and application domains emerging continuously. Understanding these trends is essential for organizations planning long-term compound AI strategies and preparing for future opportunities.

Advanced Integration Architectures

Next-generation compound AI systems are incorporating increasingly sophisticated integration architectures that enable more seamless and efficient coordination between different AI technologies.

Unified AI Platforms are emerging that provide integrated environments for developing, deploying, and managing compound AI systems. These platforms abstract away much of the complexity of technology integration while providing sophisticated orchestration capabilities.

Microservices Architectures for AI enable more flexible and scalable compound systems by decomposing AI capabilities into small, independent services that can be combined and recombined as needed.

Event-Driven Architectures enable more responsive and efficient compound AI systems by allowing different components to react to events and changes in real-time rather than requiring constant polling or coordination.

Autonomous System Orchestration

Future compound AI systems are developing increasingly sophisticated capabilities for autonomous orchestration and self-optimization, reducing the need for manual configuration and management.

Self-Organizing Systems can automatically discover and integrate new AI capabilities, optimize resource allocation, and adapt to changing requirements without human intervention.

Adaptive Load Balancing enables compound AI systems to automatically distribute workloads across different components based on current performance, resource availability, and optimization objectives.

Intelligent Caching and Optimization strategies enable compound systems to learn from usage patterns and automatically optimize performance through intelligent data management and processing strategies.

Emerging Application Domains

New application domains for compound AI are emerging as the technology matures and integration approaches become more sophisticated.

Autonomous Cities represent large-scale compound AI systems that integrate transportation, energy, communication, and governance systems to optimize urban operations and citizen services.

Personalized Medicine platforms use compound AI to integrate genetic analysis, medical imaging, treatment planning, and patient monitoring to provide comprehensive, individualized healthcare.

Intelligent Manufacturing Ecosystems combine compound AI across entire supply chains, from raw material sourcing through production, distribution, and customer service, creating end-to-end optimization and adaptation.

Embracing the Convergence Revolution

The convergence of AI technologies represents the next frontier in artificial intelligence, creating compound systems that deliver capabilities far beyond what any individual technology could achieve alone. This convergence is not just a technical evolution—it's a fundamental transformation that will reshape how we think about intelligence, automation, and human-AI collaboration.

Organizations that successfully implement compound AI capabilities are achieving unprecedented competitive advantages through improved performance, reduced costs, and entirely new capabilities that were previously impossible. The synergistic effects of technology convergence create value that exceeds the sum of individual components while enabling applications that address complex real-world challenges.

However, realizing the full potential of compound AI requires more than simply connecting different AI technologies. It requires sophisticated system design, careful attention to integration challenges, and systematic approaches to managing complexity while ensuring reliable operation. Organizations must also address the unique challenges of compound systems, including increased technical complexity, operational overhead, and strategic considerations.

The future of compound AI is bright, with emerging capabilities that will enable even more sophisticated applications and use cases. Organizations that invest in building compound AI capabilities today will be well-positioned to take advantage of these future developments while addressing challenges that no single AI technology can solve effectively.

The choice is clear: embrace the convergence revolution and unlock the transformative potential of compound AI systems, or risk being left behind by organizations that do. The technology is ready, the applications are proven, and the benefits are substantial for those bold enough to pursue them. The age of compound intelligence has begun, and the organizations that master this convergence will shape the future of AI and business.

The Implementation Blueprint - Your Roadmap to AI Transformation

"Success in AI transformation is not about having the best technology—it's about having the best strategy, the clearest roadmap, and the most systematic approach to implementation. The organizations that will dominate the AI-driven future are those that master the art of strategic execution."

In the boardroom of a Fortune 500 manufacturing company, CEO Maria Rodriguez faces a decision that will determine her company's future. Spread across the conference table are proposals for AI implementations that could transform every aspect of their operations: AI agents for supply chain optimization, multimodal AI for quality control, generative AI for product design, edge AI for real-time manufacturing control, and small language models for global workforce communication. The potential is enormous, but so is the complexity. Where should they start? How should they prioritize? What's the optimal sequence for implementation?

This scenario plays out in boardrooms around the world every day, as leaders grapple with the challenge of transforming their organizations through AI while managing risk, ensuring ROI, and maintaining operational continuity. The difference between success and failure often lies not in the choice of technology, but in the quality of the implementation strategy and the systematic execution of a well-designed roadmap.

This chapter provides the comprehensive blueprint that organizations need to navigate AI transformation successfully, offering proven frameworks, detailed roadmaps, and practical guidance based on the experiences of organizations that have achieved remarkable results through strategic AI implementation.

The Strategic Foundation: Building for Transformation Success

Successful AI transformation begins long before the first algorithm is deployed or the first model is trained. It starts with establishing a strategic foundation that aligns AI initiatives with business objectives, ensures organizational readiness, and creates the conditions for sustainable success.

Vision and Strategy Alignment

The most successful AI transformations begin with a clear, compelling vision that connects AI capabilities to specific business outcomes and competitive advantages. This vision must be more than a technology roadmap—it must articulate how AI will fundamentally change how the organization creates value, serves customers, and competes in the marketplace.

Microsoft's AI transformation provides a compelling example of vision-driven implementation [131]. CEO Satya Nadella articulated a clear vision of AI as a platform for empowering every person and organization on the planet to achieve more. This vision guided every aspect of their AI strategy, from product development to customer engagement to internal operations.

The strategic alignment process involves several critical components: defining specific business outcomes that AI will enable, identifying competitive advantages that AI capabilities will create, establishing success metrics that connect AI performance to business value, and creating governance structures that ensure AI initiatives remain aligned with strategic objectives.

Organizations that achieve the strongest results from AI transformation report that 73% of their success comes from strategic clarity and organizational alignment, while only 27% comes from technology selection and implementation. This finding underscores the critical importance of getting the strategic foundation right before focusing on technical implementation.

Organizational Readiness Assessment

Before embarking on AI transformation, organizations must honestly assess their readiness across multiple dimensions: technical infrastructure, data maturity, organizational capabilities, cultural factors, and change management capacity. This assessment provides the foundation for developing realistic timelines, identifying capability gaps, and designing appropriate implementation strategies.

Technical Infrastructure Assessment evaluates the organization's current technology stack, data architecture, computational resources, and integration capabilities. Many organizations discover that their existing infrastructure requires significant upgrades to support advanced AI applications effectively.

Data Maturity Evaluation examines the quality, accessibility, governance, and usability of organizational data. AI systems are only as good as the data they're trained on, making data readiness a critical success factor for AI transformation.

Organizational Capabilities Analysis assesses the current skills, knowledge, and experience within the organization related to AI development, deployment, and management. Most organizations require significant capability building to support AI transformation effectively.

Cultural Readiness Evaluation examines the organization's openness to change, tolerance for experimentation, and willingness to embrace new ways of working. Cultural factors often determine whether AI initiatives succeed or fail, regardless of their technical merit.

Governance and Risk Management Framework

AI transformation requires sophisticated governance frameworks that balance innovation with risk management, ensure ethical AI development and deployment, and maintain compliance with evolving regulatory requirements. These frameworks must be established early in the transformation process and evolved continuously as AI capabilities mature.

AI Ethics and Responsible AI principles provide the foundation for ensuring that AI systems are developed and deployed in ways that are fair, transparent, accountable, and beneficial to all stakeholders. Organizations must establish clear guidelines for AI ethics and embed these principles throughout their AI development and deployment processes.

Risk Management Frameworks must address the unique risks associated with AI systems, including algorithmic bias, data privacy, security vulnerabilities, and operational dependencies. These frameworks should include risk assessment procedures, mitigation strategies, and monitoring systems.

Compliance and Regulatory Considerations become increasingly important as AI regulations evolve worldwide. Organizations must stay current with regulatory developments and ensure their AI systems comply with applicable laws and standards.

Quality Assurance and Validation procedures ensure that AI systems meet performance, reliability, and safety standards before deployment. These procedures must address both technical performance and business impact validation.

The Four-Phase Implementation Framework

Based on analysis of hundreds of successful AI transformations across industries, a clear pattern emerges: the most successful implementations follow a systematic four-phase approach that builds capabilities incrementally while demonstrating value at each stage. This framework provides a proven roadmap for organizations of all sizes and industries.

Phase 1: Foundation and Strategy (Months 1-6)

The first phase focuses on establishing the strategic, organizational, and technical foundations necessary for successful AI transformation. This phase is critical for ensuring that subsequent implementation efforts are built on solid ground and aligned with business objectives.

Strategic Planning and Vision Development involves creating a comprehensive AI strategy that aligns with business objectives, identifies priority use cases, and establishes success metrics. This includes conducting market analysis, competitive assessment, and opportunity identification to ensure the AI strategy creates sustainable competitive advantages.

Organizational Assessment and Capability Building includes evaluating current capabilities, identifying skill gaps, and developing training and hiring plans to build necessary AI expertise. Most organizations require significant capability building during this phase, including technical skills, project management capabilities, and change management expertise.

Infrastructure Planning and Preparation involves assessing current technical infrastructure, identifying upgrade requirements, and beginning the process of building the technical foundation needed to support AI applications. This often includes cloud migration, data platform modernization, and security enhancement initiatives.

Governance Framework Development establishes the policies, procedures, and organizational structures needed to manage AI initiatives effectively. This includes creating AI ethics guidelines, risk management procedures, and quality assurance frameworks.

Data Strategy and Preparation focuses on assessing data readiness, implementing data governance procedures, and beginning the process of preparing data for AI applications. This often represents one of the most time-consuming aspects of AI transformation but is essential for success.

Pilot Use Case Selection involves identifying and prioritizing initial AI applications that can demonstrate value while building organizational confidence and expertise. The best pilot use cases typically have clear success metrics, manageable scope, and high potential impact.

Phase 2: Pilot Implementation and Learning (Months 4-12)

The second phase involves implementing pilot AI applications to validate the approach, demonstrate value, and build organizational confidence and expertise. This phase is designed to achieve early wins while learning lessons that will inform broader implementation efforts.

Pilot Development and Deployment focuses on building and deploying the selected pilot applications using agile development methodologies that enable rapid iteration and learning. Pilots should be designed to test not just technical capabilities but also organizational processes and change management approaches.

Performance Measurement and Validation involves establishing comprehensive metrics for evaluating pilot success, including technical performance, business impact, user satisfaction, and organizational learning. These metrics provide the foundation for making informed decisions about scaling AI initiatives.

Stakeholder Engagement and Change Management ensures that affected stakeholders understand the AI initiatives, are prepared for changes to their work, and are equipped to contribute to successful implementation. This includes training programs, communication initiatives, and feedback collection processes.

Process Integration and Workflow Design involves integrating AI capabilities into existing business processes and workflows, often requiring significant process redesign to realize the full benefits of AI automation and augmentation.

Quality Assurance and Risk Management procedures are tested and refined during pilot implementation, ensuring that quality and risk management frameworks are effective before broader deployment.

Learning Capture and Knowledge Transfer processes ensure that lessons learned during pilot implementation are documented and shared across the organization to inform future AI initiatives.

Phase 3: Scale and Expand (Months 9-24)

The third phase involves scaling successful pilot applications and expanding AI capabilities across the organization. This phase requires sophisticated program management, change management, and technical coordination to ensure successful scaling while maintaining quality and performance.

Scaling Strategy Development involves planning how to expand successful AI applications across the organization while managing complexity, resource requirements, and change management challenges. This includes prioritizing expansion opportunities, planning resource allocation, and designing scaling approaches.

Platform and Infrastructure Scaling ensures that technical infrastructure can support expanded AI applications while maintaining performance, reliability, and security. This often requires significant infrastructure investment and sophisticated capacity planning.

Organizational Capability Expansion involves scaling training programs, hiring additional AI talent, and building the organizational capabilities needed to support expanded AI operations. This includes developing internal AI expertise and establishing centers of excellence.

Process Standardization and Optimization involves standardizing successful AI implementation approaches, optimizing workflows and processes, and establishing best practices that can be applied across the organization.

Quality and Performance Management systems are expanded to monitor AI applications at scale, ensuring consistent performance and identifying optimization opportunities across the AI portfolio.

Change Management and Adoption Support programs are scaled to support organization-wide AI adoption, including training, communication, and support systems that help employees adapt to AI-enhanced work environments.

Phase 4: Optimize and Transform (Months 18-36+)

The fourth phase involves optimizing AI applications for maximum impact and using AI capabilities to fundamentally transform business models, customer experiences, and competitive positioning. This phase represents the transition from AI adoption to AI-driven transformation.

Advanced Capability Development involves building sophisticated AI applications that leverage multiple technologies, address complex business challenges, and create significant competitive advantages. This often includes compound AI systems that integrate multiple AI technologies.

Business Model Innovation uses AI capabilities to create new products, services, and business models that weren't previously possible. This may include new revenue streams, customer experiences, and value propositions enabled by AI.

Ecosystem Integration involves extending AI capabilities beyond organizational boundaries to include partners, suppliers, and customers in AI-enhanced ecosystems. This creates network effects and competitive moats that are difficult for competitors to replicate.

Continuous Innovation and Improvement establishes processes for continuously evolving AI capabilities, staying current with technological developments, and maintaining competitive advantages through ongoing innovation.

Strategic Advantage Realization involves leveraging AI capabilities to achieve sustainable competitive advantages, market leadership, and superior business performance that justifies the investment in AI transformation.

Cultural Transformation ensures that AI-driven ways of working become embedded in organizational culture, enabling sustained innovation and adaptation as AI technologies continue to evolve.

Industry-Specific Implementation Strategies

While the four-phase framework provides a general roadmap for AI transformation, different industries face unique challenges, opportunities, and constraints that require tailored implementation approaches. Understanding these industry-specific considerations is essential for developing effective AI transformation strategies.

Healthcare: Regulatory Compliance and Patient Safety

Healthcare organizations face unique challenges in AI implementation due to strict regulatory requirements, patient safety considerations, and complex clinical workflows. Successful healthcare AI implementations require specialized approaches that address these constraints while realizing the significant potential benefits.

Regulatory Compliance Strategy must address FDA approval processes, HIPAA privacy requirements, and clinical validation standards that are unique to healthcare. AI applications in healthcare often require extensive clinical trials and regulatory approval before deployment, significantly extending implementation timelines.

Clinical Integration Approach involves working closely with healthcare providers to integrate AI capabilities into clinical workflows without disrupting patient care. This requires deep understanding of clinical processes and extensive stakeholder engagement with medical professionals.

Patient Safety and Quality Assurance procedures must meet the highest standards, as AI errors in healthcare can have life-threatening consequences. This includes extensive testing, validation, and monitoring procedures that exceed requirements in other industries.

Data Privacy and Security considerations are particularly stringent in healthcare due to the sensitive nature of medical data and strict regulatory requirements. Healthcare AI implementations require sophisticated data protection and privacy preservation techniques.

Mayo Clinic's AI implementation provides an excellent example of healthcare-specific AI transformation [133]. Their approach emphasizes clinical validation, regulatory compliance, and seamless integration with clinical workflows while maintaining the highest standards for patient safety and data privacy.

Financial Services: Risk Management and Regulatory Oversight

Financial services organizations operate in highly regulated environments with strict risk management requirements and extensive oversight. AI implementations in financial services must address these constraints while delivering the significant benefits possible in areas like fraud detection, risk assessment, and customer service.

Regulatory Compliance Framework must address banking regulations, securities laws, and consumer protection requirements that vary by jurisdiction and business line. Financial services AI implementations often require regulatory approval and ongoing oversight.

Risk Management Integration involves incorporating AI capabilities into existing risk management frameworks while ensuring that AI systems themselves don't introduce unacceptable risks. This includes model validation, stress testing, and ongoing monitoring procedures.

Algorithmic Fairness and Bias Prevention are particularly important in financial services due to fair lending laws and consumer protection requirements. AI systems must be designed and monitored to ensure fair treatment of all customers.

Data Governance and Privacy procedures must meet strict financial services standards while enabling AI applications that require access to sensitive customer and transaction data.

JPMorgan Chase's AI transformation demonstrates effective financial services AI implementation [134]. Their approach emphasizes regulatory compliance, risk management, and algorithmic fairness while achieving significant improvements in fraud detection, customer service, and operational efficiency.

Manufacturing: Operational Integration and Safety

Manufacturing organizations face unique challenges in AI implementation due to complex operational environments, safety requirements, and the need to integrate AI with existing industrial systems. Successful manufacturing AI implementations require specialized approaches that address these operational constraints.

Operational Technology Integration involves connecting AI systems with existing manufacturing equipment, control systems, and operational processes. This often requires significant technical integration work and careful coordination with operational teams.

Safety and Reliability Requirements in manufacturing environments are particularly stringent, as AI failures can result in equipment damage, production disruptions, or safety incidents. Manufacturing AI implementations require extensive testing and validation procedures.

Production Continuity considerations ensure that AI implementations don't disrupt ongoing production operations. This often requires phased implementation approaches and extensive contingency planning.

Workforce Integration and Training programs help manufacturing workers adapt to AI-enhanced production environments while maintaining safety and quality standards.

Siemens' smart manufacturing initiatives provide an excellent example of manufacturing AI transformation. Their approach emphasizes operational integration, safety, and workforce development while achieving significant improvements in efficiency, quality, and sustainability.

Retail: Customer Experience and Operational Efficiency

Retail organizations face unique opportunities and challenges in AI implementation due to direct customer interactions, complex supply chains, and rapidly changing market conditions. Successful retail AI implementations must balance customer experience enhancement with operational efficiency improvements.

Customer Experience Integration involves implementing AI capabilities that enhance customer interactions without creating friction or privacy concerns. This includes personalization, recommendation systems, and customer service automation.

Omnichannel Integration ensures that AI capabilities work seamlessly across online and offline channels, providing consistent customer experiences regardless of how customers choose to interact with the retailer.

Supply Chain Optimization uses AI to improve inventory management, demand forecasting, and logistics operations while maintaining customer service levels and managing costs.

Privacy and Personalization Balance involves using customer data to provide personalized experiences while respecting privacy preferences and complying with data protection regulations.

Amazon's retail AI implementation demonstrates effective retail AI transformation [136]. Their approach emphasizes customer experience, operational efficiency, and continuous innovation while maintaining privacy and building customer trust.

Technology-Specific Implementation Considerations

Each of the five AI technologies requires specific implementation approaches that address their unique characteristics, requirements, and integration challenges. Understanding these technology-specific considerations is essential for successful implementation.

AI Agents Implementation Strategy

AI agents require sophisticated implementation approaches that address their autonomous nature, decision-making capabilities, and integration with existing systems and processes.

Autonomy and Control Balance involves designing AI agents that can operate autonomously while maintaining appropriate human oversight and control. This requires careful consideration of decision boundaries, escalation procedures, and override mechanisms.

Integration Architecture must enable AI agents to interact with existing systems, access necessary data, and coordinate with other AI and non-AI systems. This often requires significant API development and system integration work.

Performance Monitoring and Management systems must track AI agent behavior, decision quality, and business impact while providing mechanisms for continuous improvement and optimization.

Trust and Transparency mechanisms help users understand AI agent decisions and build confidence in autonomous systems. This includes explainability features, audit trails, and performance reporting.

Multimodal AI Implementation Strategy

Multimodal AI systems require specialized implementation approaches that address their complex data requirements, processing needs, and integration challenges.

Data Pipeline Architecture must handle multiple data types simultaneously while ensuring quality, consistency, and performance. This often requires sophisticated data engineering and processing capabilities.

Model Integration and Coordination involves combining different AI models that process different data types while maintaining coherence and consistency across modalities.

Performance Optimization addresses the computational complexity of multimodal processing while meeting latency and throughput requirements for real-time applications.

Quality Assurance and Validation procedures must address the unique challenges of multimodal systems, including cross-modal consistency, accuracy across different data types, and overall system performance.

Generative AI Implementation Strategy

Generative AI implementations require careful attention to quality control, content governance, and creative workflow integration.

Content Quality and Control systems ensure that generated content meets organizational standards for accuracy, appropriateness, and brand consistency. This includes review processes, quality metrics, and automated filtering systems.

Creative Workflow Integration involves incorporating generative AI into existing creative processes while maintaining quality standards and creative control. This often requires significant process redesign and stakeholder engagement.

Intellectual Property and Legal Considerations address the unique legal challenges associated with AI-generated content, including copyright, attribution, and liability issues.

Scalability and Performance Management ensures that generative AI systems can handle production workloads while maintaining quality and performance standards.

Edge AI Implementation Strategy

Edge AI implementations require specialized approaches that address resource constraints, deployment complexity, and management challenges.

Resource Optimization involves designing AI systems that can operate effectively within the computational, memory, and power constraints of edge devices. This often requires model compression, optimization, and specialized hardware selection.

Deployment and Management strategies must address the challenges of deploying and maintaining AI systems across potentially thousands of edge devices with varying connectivity and accessibility.

Security and Privacy considerations are particularly important for edge AI systems that may operate in unsecured environments or handle sensitive data locally.

Performance Monitoring and Maintenance procedures must work effectively with limited connectivity and remote deployment scenarios while ensuring consistent performance across distributed systems.

Small Language Models Implementation Strategy

Small language model implementations require approaches that balance efficiency with capability while addressing deployment and integration challenges.

Efficiency Optimization involves selecting and optimizing small language models for specific use cases while maintaining acceptable performance within resource constraints.

Domain Specialization strategies focus small language models on specific applications or industries to maximize performance while maintaining efficiency.

Integration and Deployment approaches must address the unique characteristics of small language models while ensuring seamless integration with existing systems and workflows.

Continuous Learning and Adaptation mechanisms enable small language models to improve over time while operating within resource constraints and deployment limitations.

Measuring Success: KPIs and ROI Frameworks

Successful AI transformation requires comprehensive measurement frameworks that track progress, demonstrate value, and guide optimization efforts. These frameworks must address both technical performance and business impact while providing actionable insights for continuous improvement.

Technical Performance Metrics

Technical performance metrics provide the foundation for evaluating AI system effectiveness and identifying optimization opportunities. These metrics must be tailored to specific AI technologies and applications while providing consistent measurement across the AI portfolio.

Accuracy and Quality Metrics measure how well AI systems perform their intended functions, including prediction accuracy, content quality, decision effectiveness, and error rates. These metrics must be specific to each AI application while enabling comparison across different systems.

Performance and Efficiency Metrics track computational performance, response times, throughput, and resource utilization to ensure AI systems meet operational requirements while optimizing costs.

Reliability and Availability Metrics monitor system uptime, failure rates, and recovery times to ensure AI systems provide consistent, dependable service that meets business requirements.

Scalability and Capacity Metrics track how well AI systems handle increasing workloads and usage while maintaining performance and quality standards.

Business Impact Metrics

Business impact metrics connect AI performance to business outcomes, demonstrating the value of AI investments and guiding strategic decisions about AI initiatives.

Revenue Impact Metrics track how AI systems contribute to revenue generation through improved sales, new products and services, enhanced customer experiences, and market expansion opportunities.

Cost Reduction Metrics measure how AI systems reduce operational costs through automation, efficiency improvements, error reduction, and resource optimization.

Productivity and Efficiency Metrics track how AI systems improve employee productivity, process efficiency, and operational effectiveness across different business functions.

Customer Experience Metrics monitor how AI systems impact customer satisfaction, engagement, retention, and loyalty while identifying opportunities for improvement.

Quality and Risk Metrics measure how AI systems improve product and service quality while reducing operational, financial, and reputational risks.

ROI Calculation Framework

Return on investment calculation for AI initiatives requires sophisticated frameworks that account for both direct and indirect benefits while considering implementation costs, ongoing operational expenses, and opportunity costs.

Direct Cost Components include technology licensing, infrastructure investments, development costs, training expenses, and ongoing operational costs. These costs must be tracked comprehensively to ensure accurate ROI calculation.

Direct Benefit Components include revenue increases, cost reductions, productivity improvements, and risk mitigation that can be directly attributed to AI implementations. These benefits must be measured accurately and validated through appropriate controls.

Indirect Benefit Components include strategic advantages, competitive positioning improvements, innovation acceleration, and capability building that provide long-term value but may be difficult to quantify precisely.

Time-Based Analysis tracks how AI benefits and costs evolve over time, including initial investment periods, ramp-up phases, steady-state operations, and long-term strategic value realization.

Risk-Adjusted Returns account for the uncertainty and risk associated with AI investments while providing realistic expectations for investment returns and payback periods.

Change Management and Organizational Transformation

AI transformation is fundamentally an organizational transformation that requires sophisticated change management approaches to ensure successful adoption and sustained value realization. The human and cultural aspects of AI transformation are often more challenging than the technical aspects and require dedicated attention and resources.

Stakeholder Engagement and Communication

Effective stakeholder engagement is critical for AI transformation success, as AI initiatives typically affect multiple organizational functions and require broad support for successful implementation.

Leadership Alignment and Sponsorship ensures that senior leaders understand, support, and actively champion AI transformation initiatives. This includes regular communication, progress reporting, and strategic alignment activities.

Employee Engagement and Participation involves employees in AI transformation planning and implementation while addressing concerns about job displacement, skill requirements, and changing work environments.

Customer Communication and Education helps customers understand how AI enhancements will improve their experiences while addressing privacy concerns and building trust in AI-powered services.

Partner and Supplier Engagement extends AI transformation benefits to ecosystem partners while ensuring alignment and coordination across organizational boundaries.

Training and Capability Building

AI transformation requires significant investment in training and capability building to ensure that employees can work effectively with AI systems and contribute to ongoing AI innovation.

Technical Skills Development provides employees with the technical knowledge needed to work with AI systems, including data analysis, model interpretation, and system operation skills.

Business Skills Enhancement helps employees understand how to leverage AI capabilities for business value while developing skills in AI-human collaboration and decision-making.

Leadership Development prepares managers and executives to lead AI-driven organizations while making informed decisions about AI investments and strategies.

Continuous Learning Programs ensure that employees stay current with evolving AI capabilities while developing new skills needed for AI-enhanced work environments.

Cultural Transformation

AI transformation requires cultural changes that embrace experimentation, data-driven decision-making, and continuous learning while maintaining human values and organizational purpose.

Innovation Culture Development encourages experimentation, risk-taking, and learning from failure while maintaining appropriate governance and risk management.

Data-Driven Decision Making embeds analytical thinking and evidence-based decision-making throughout the organization while maintaining human judgment and intuition.

Collaboration and Transparency promote open communication, knowledge sharing, and cross-functional collaboration that are essential for AI transformation success.

Ethical AI Culture ensures that AI development and deployment align with organizational values and ethical principles while promoting responsible AI practices.

Conclusion: Your Path to AI Leadership

The implementation of AI transformation is not just a technological journey—it's a strategic imperative that will determine organizational success in the AI-driven future. The frameworks, strategies, and roadmaps presented in this chapter provide a comprehensive blueprint for navigating this transformation successfully while avoiding common pitfalls and maximizing value realization.

The organizations that will lead in the AI era are those that approach transformation systematically, with clear strategies, proven frameworks, and unwavering commitment to execution excellence. They understand that AI transformation is not about implementing technology—it's about reimagining how organizations create value, serve customers, and compete in rapidly evolving markets.

The four-phase implementation framework provides a proven roadmap that has guided hundreds of successful AI transformations across industries and organizational sizes. By following this systematic approach while adapting to industry-specific requirements and organizational constraints, leaders can navigate the complexity of AI transformation while building sustainable competitive advantages.

Success in AI transformation requires more than technical expertise—it demands strategic thinking, organizational leadership, and change management excellence. The measurement frameworks and success metrics provide the tools needed to track progress, demonstrate value, and guide optimization efforts throughout the transformation journey.

The choice facing every organization today is not whether to embrace AI transformation, but how quickly and effectively they can execute it. The frameworks and strategies in this chapter provide the roadmap for success, but execution depends on leadership commitment, organizational alignment, and systematic implementation.

Appendix A
Key Terms & Glossary

A brief guide to key concepts from across the book—designed for reference, review, and continued clarity.

AI Agent

A system that can perceive its environment, make decisions, and take autonomous actions toward defined goals. Examples include virtual assistants, autonomous vehicles, and logistics bots.

Multimodal AI

AI that integrates multiple types of input—like text, image, audio, and video—into a single system to interpret context and respond more naturally, similar to human perception.

Generative AI

A class of AI models capable of creating original content—text, images, music, video, code, etc.—using learned patterns. Includes LLMs, GANs, and diffusion models.

Large Language Model (LLM)

A deep learning model trained on massive text corpora to predict and generate language. Examples: GPT-4, PaLM, Claude.

Small Language Model (SLM)

A more compact version of an LLM designed for faster, private, and often offline use. Examples: Mistral, LLaMA 2, Phi.

Edge AI

AI processing that occurs on local devices—like phones, drones, or IoT sensors—rather than relying on cloud-based servers. Enables real-time, private, and low-latency responses.

Diffusion Model

A generative model that starts with random noise and gradually transforms it into coherent outputs (e.g., images), like sculpting order from chaos.

GAN (Generative Adversarial Network)

A type of generative model where two neural networks—generator and discriminator—compete to create and refine realistic data outputs.

Knowledge Distillation

A technique where a smaller model learns to replicate the behavior of a larger model, like a student learning from an expert's summary notes.

Quantization

Compressing an AI model by reducing numerical precision, similar to shrinking a high-res photo while maintaining clarity—used to run models on limited hardware.

Federated Learning

A decentralized training approach where models learn from data stored on edge devices without centralizing sensitive information—enabling collaborative improvement while protecting privacy.

LoRA (Low-Rank Adaptation)

A method for fine-tuning language models efficiently using smaller data updates, allowing rapid, lightweight customization.

Appendix B
Further Reading & Resources

To deepen your understanding, explore the resources below—curated across disciplines, formats, and perspectives.

Books

- Rebooting AI – Gary Marcus & Ernest Davis
- Tools and Weapons – Brad Smith & Carol Ann Browne
- The Alignment Problem – Brian Christian
- The Coming Wave – Mustafa Suleyman
- AI Superpowers – Kai-Fu Lee

Key Reports and Frameworks

- OECD AI Principles
- EU AI Act (Regulatory Framework)
- NIST Risk Management Framework for AI
- UNESCO Recommendation on the Ethics of AI
- Stanford AI Index Report (Annual)

Open Source Model Hubs

- Hugging Face[1] – Repository for LLMs, SLMs, and community models

- EleutherAI[2] – Research and models focused on transparency and openness

- Mistral.ai[3] – Open-weight language models optimized for efficiency

Courses and Learning Platforms

- Elements of AI – Free course by University of Helsinki

- Fast.ai – Practical deep learning for coders

- MIT OpenCourseWare – Artificial Intelligence

- DeepLearning.AI – Specializations on LLMs, multimodal, and generative models

Communities and Think Tanks

- Partnership on AI – Cross-sector collaboration on responsible AI

- AI Now Institute – Social implications and policy development

---

1. https://huggingface.co

2. https://www.eleuther.ai

3. https://mistral.ai

- Center for Humane Technology – Human-first tech design
- Data & Society Research Institute – Intersection of data, AI, and culture

Let this appendix serve as your compass for further exploration.

The most important chapter of this revolution is still being written—by you.

The future belongs to organizations that master AI transformation. The blueprint is clear, the path is proven, and the opportunity is unprecedented. The only question remaining is: will you lead the transformation or be transformed by it?

Did you love *The Fifth Intelligence Five Foundational Technologies Defining the 21st Century*? Then you should read *The Data Whisperer: See the Patterns*[4] by Kala Montena!

[5]

Title: ***The Data Whisperer***

See the Patterns. Break the Loop. Reclaim Your Life

Your Guide to Thriving in a Data-Driven World

In a world shaped by invisible algorithms, are you truly choosing-or simply reacting?

The Data Whisperer is a groundbreaking, soul-stirring guide to understanding the hidden forces shaping your decisions, habits, identity, and future. Blending behavioral psychology, digital anthropology, neuroscience, and sacred wisdom, Kala Montena

---

4. https://books2read.com/u/bxXMDo

5. https://books2read.com/u/bxXMDo

delivers a masterwork that's both deeply personal and powerfully practical.

This book isn't about learning to code-it's about learning to see.

You'll discover how algorithms track your every move, how data brokers build hidden profiles of you, and how social media platforms hijack your attention. But more importantly, you'll gain the tools to reclaim your mind, protect your privacy, and become the author of your own digital life.

Inside, You'll Learn:

How algorithmic bias and behavioral design shape what you believeWhy your digital footprint matters more than you thinkTools to audit your data trail and protect your identityPractices to reclaim focus in an age of distractionStrategies to navigate the attention economy with integrityHow to raise data-conscious children in a hyperconnected world

Perfect For Readers Who Love:

Digital Minimalism by Cal Newport*The Age of Surveillance Capitalism* by Shoshana Zuboff*Stolen Focus* by Johann Hari*Atomic Habits* by James Clear*The Psychology of Influence* by Robert Cialdini

Whether you're a student, parent, entrepreneur, educator, or everyday citizen, this book offers a clear, compassionate path to digital clarity and self-empowerment.

www.ingramcontent.com/pod-product-compliance
Lightning Source LLC
LaVergne TN
LVHW090405210926
848480LV00002B/456